Coping
with Stress
at University

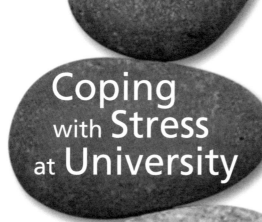

Coping
with Stress
at University

a Survival
Guide

Stephen Palmer
& Angela Puri

SAGE Publications
London ● Thousand Oaks ● New Delhi

378.198

 SAGE Publications Ltd
1 Oliver's Yard
55 City Road
London EC1Y 1SP

SAGE Publications Inc.
2455 Teller Road
Thousand Oaks, California 91320

SAGE Publications India Pvt Ltd
B-42, Panchsheel Enclave
Post Box 4109
New Delhi 110 017

British Library Cataloguing in Publication data

A catalogue record for this book is available
from the British Library

ISBN10 1 4129 0732 2   ISBN13 978 1 4129 0732 3
ISBN10 1 4129 0733 0 (pbk)   ISBN13 978 1 4129 0733 0

Library of Congress Control Number: 2005929761

Typeset by C&M Digitals (P) Ltd., Chennai, India
Printed on paper from sustainable resources
Printed in Great Britain by The Cromwell Press Ltd, Trowbridge, Wiltshire

To Maggie,
Kate, Kevin and Joshua
Tom and Arina
And all the students I've taught since 1982
(SP)

To mum and dad: for all your
guidance and support;
And to Reehan: for your positivity,
patience and for being you!
(AP)

Contents

Acknowledgements

We would like to thank Professor Cary Cooper for the reproduction of the Type A, Locus of Control and Coping with Stress questionnaires, and the Department of Health for allowing us to reproduce their material. We would like to thank staff at Sage Publications for their support, in particular, our Senior Editor Patrick Brindle.

(SP & AP)

Thank you to all the students who contributed to the case studies provided in the book and a special thank you to Adi, Neelu, Sandy, Shilpen, Atul, Poonum, and Alex for all their help and support. And finally thanks to Steve for giving me the opportunity!

(AP)

A quick introduction

Stress and university. These are not two words you often see together! Many people recollect university as being the *'best days of their lives'* or *'a great laugh'* and we hope that this will be the case for you too.

However, university is associated with huge change, and for most people change brings stress. At university there is a need to be more proactive in your studies, your social life and your ability to manage on your own. Although this transition is often depicted as being good fun, many students have difficulty in dealing with the fine balance between freedom and autonomy coupled with self-reliance and being financially independent.

Starting university often means leaving family and friends and entering an unfamiliar environment, where you need to establish yourself afresh. Furthermore, many students find the change in teaching style is considerably different from the way national schools and colleges administer lessons. The style of lectures may leave some students feeling a little bewildered.

Although stress at university is not often talked about, a recent survey (MORI, 2005), found that 58 per cent of students indicated that *'since being a student I feel under a lot more stress than before'*. In addition, student counselling services have observed a rise in the proportion of students that they see and the number of students exhibiting signs of 'severe distress' is rising every year (Association of University and College Counselling, 2001).

But do not despair! Although stress is appearing more frequently on the student agenda, 95 per cent of students feel that going to university is a *'worthwhile experience'*, and that they are *'happy with life'* (88 per cent). In addition, two-thirds of students suggest that the best part of the student experience is *'the freedom to live how I want'* (MORI, 2005).

For the new student, university can bring forth a number of different feelings and emotions, as you are exposed to a whole host of new experiences and challenges. This handbook aims to provide you with an insight into the various aspects of student life and how to cope effectively with the stress that these changes may bring.

How to use this handbook

Everyone is different and the issues and concerns of each student will naturally vary. This handbook has been written with this in mind, with each chapter covering a different aspect of university life and the potential stress relating to that area. So the handbook enables you to dip into any chapter quickly to learn tips and techniques to help you.

Alternatively, as the handbook is quite compact, it will also make a relatively quick read. You can either work through the whole book for an overview and then later return and practise techniques, or just pick out sections you require if and when you need them.

The aim of this handbook differs from many books available on life at university. It is not written to advise you on what is right or wrong but to identify situations and highlight techniques that will help you survive the stress of university. The book takes a self-coaching approach whereby we provide you with the skills and knowledge to help you along the way!

Please note: For the techniques to be effective practise will be required.

Each chapter finishes with a review for you to fill in. This is to help you note down any problems you wish to deal with and useful strategies within the chapter that will help you to manage your own stress. By the end of the handbook you will have enough information on the problems that you associate as being stressful to develop your own action plan to overcome them. Although many of the techniques outlined in the book are there to help you survive the stress of university, they are not limited to the university experience. Once you learn these skills, you will be better equipped to deal with stress throughout your life.

Finally, it is important to emphasise that this handbook is a guide and should not be used instead of counselling or other help services. If you do feel that you may need help with a particular issue, a number of relevant resources are mentioned at the end of each chapter and there is also a comprehensive list of counselling and advice agencies in Appendix 2.

Before you begin

Before you begin reading this handbook, it may be useful to think about what you want to achieve by reading it. Once you are aware of what your main goals are, you are likely to be more focused on achieving them. By doing the exercise below, you will also find it easier to identify strategies or techniques which are relevant and effective for assisting you with your personal pressures and stress.

Have a go! Goals and objectives

List the goals or objectives that you would like this handbook to help you with. The aim of this exercise is to help you gain an understanding of *what* you want to achieve. The handbook should then help you understand *how* to achieve it!

- Goal 1:

- Goal 2:

- Goal 3:

- Goal 4:

- Goal 5:

Part 1   What is stress?

Although you may hear the word 'stress' used all the time, if you were asked to explain what stress actually means, you may find that it is a harder question to answer than you originally thought!

This section of the handbook explores the different interpretations of the word 'stress' and how your own perception of the world around you influences your definition of the term. In addition, the body's reaction to stress is also discussed in detail (the stress response) and you have the opportunity to fill in a questionnaire to identify how your own body reacts in stressful situations.

As the perception of what is stressful differs from person to person, Part 1 of the handbook gives you an insight into your own stress levels. There are questionnaires which allow you to identify how you handle your day-to-day problems (The Life Stress questionnaire), what your personality type is (Type A or Type B questionnaire) and the views you hold about the world around you and the amount of control you believe you have over circumstances and events which occur in your life (Locus of Control questionnaire).

By the time you have completed Part 1 of the handbook, you will have a greater awareness of what situations in your life may cause you stress and you will also be able to identify how stress impacts on your psychological and physical well-being.

1

Understanding stress

What this chapter covers

In this introductory chapter, we define what is meant by the word 'stress' and why it is a term that is so hard to conceptualise. The chapter looks at how stress affects your health and explains the long-term repercussions of ignoring the warning signs your body provides when you are stressed. There is also an exercise at the end of the chapter for you to identify how you react when you are feeling the pressure.

What is stress?

Have you ever had one of those days where you just wanted to turn back time, crawl into bed and start the day again?

If you have, it is likely to have resulted from a number of incidences or experiences which had a negative impact on you, such as an argument with a friend or getting a poor mark in a piece of course work. When things do not appear to be going to plan, many of us begin to focus on all the negatives which are occurring. Have you ever heard yourself saying, '*everything is going wrong today*!' and if so, did you feel '*stressed*'? This type of thinking, or over-generalisation, of your problems does not necessarily make you feel better. In fact, negative thought actually makes you feel worse! By thinking that your day is truly awful, you are more likely to work yourself up into a state, where you actually increase your levels of stress.

But what do we mean by the term '*stress*'? It is a word we seem to hear almost everyday and we are constantly bombarded with media coverage telling us about the dangers of stress. Interestingly, the term 'stress' is used to refer to serious health hazards and situations, such as divorce and bereavements, as well as a range of more day-to-day scenarios, such as missing a deadline or not knowing what clothes to wear to a party! So the word itself appears to be an umbrella term, incorporating a variety of problems that may occur on a fairly regular basis, to more infrequent and serious life-changing events.

So, before we can begin to tackle ways of managing your stress, we need to explore how we define stress, understand what triggers your response to stress and how stress impacts on your day-to-day lives.

Definition of stress

One of the most commonly used definitions of stress is by Dr Richard Lazarus:

Stress arises when individuals perceive that they cannot
adequately cope with the demands being made on them or
with threats to their well-being. (Lazarus and Folkman, 1984)

It is important to note that the definition implies that it is not the actual situation which causes the stress, but the *beliefs* and *thoughts* which are held about the situation. For example, it is not necessarily the external pressure of a course work deadline which causes stress, but whether you *believe* that you can complete the course work in the time allocated.

Conversely, if you do not perceive the situation as being important or threatening to you, then regardless of whether you are successful or not at dealing with the situation, you are less likely to feel stressed. For example, if you learn that the course work you are worrying about will not count towards your final marks, you may not be as anxious to complete it by the deadline date.

This explanation of the causes of stress is fairly modern and was developed by well-known psychologists and researchers such as Dr Albert Ellis and Dr Aaron Beck in the 1950s and early 1960s. It is underpinned by much research. However, if we travel back in time, we discover stoic philosophers 2000 years ago had developed a similar model:

People are not disturbed by things but by the views which
*they take of them. (*Epictetus)

Everything is but what your opinion makes it; and that
opinion lies with yourself. (Marcus Aurelius, *Meditations*)

More recently a few centuries ago, William Shakespeare repeated this idea:

Hamlet: *Why, then 'tis none to you; for there is nothing either*
good or bad but thinking makes it so. (Hamlet, II.ii 256–61)

Of course, there are other factors that influence your stress levels when dealing with a particular situation. If you are used to managing your time and are given a tight deadline, you are less likely to feel under pressure. This would also explain how, with continued experience, a number of scenarios, such as giving a presentation or reaching deadlines, become less and less stressful. However, if you are not used to the pressure, you may believe that there is not enough time to complete the task, and this belief is likely to increase your stress levels because of the difference in the way you perceive the situation.

We have now briefly touched upon *what* stress is. However, if we are interested in tackling stress, we also need to understand the reasoning behind *why* we become stressed.

Back to basics – the stress response

You may have heard of the term 'fight or flight', which is also known as the stress response. These terms are used to explain your body's way of dealing with stressful scenarios. The response is involuntary and occurs automatically when you are faced with a situation which you perceive as threatening.

When you find yourself in a threatening or challenging situation, the body's biological mechanisms get ready for action. Your nervous system quickly comes into play, causing the body to react in the following way:

- Hormones are released that prepare different organs of the body for action
- Heart beat increases
- Blood pressure rises
- Sugar and fat levels increase to provide extra energy
- Blood is redirected from non-vital areas, such as the digestive system, to the heart and major muscles of the body
- Blood clotting time is reduced
- Pupils dilate to ensure we are more alert to the environment around us

The whole body is on a high state of alert, consuming more energy and other natural resources as the body remains ready for action.

This response is a very effective way of dealing with the types of problem or *stressor* (situations which trigger stress) that our early ancestors may have faced whilst hunting for food. However, in today's environment this is rarely an efficient way of dealing with the many problems you may face daily. This is one of the reasons why stress has become a prominent issue over the past few decades, because although the way your body reacts to stress has not evolved over time, your stressors have changed drastically. Threats are not so much physical challenges but are more likely to be threats to your sense of worth.

Your body returns to its natural state of equilibrium once you perceive that the threatening situation has passed. However, it is unlikely that a stressful situation nowadays will just *pass*; in fact, if it is not dealt with appropriately it may well accumulate over time. This is why stress is becoming such a health hazard. If the perceived problem isn't altered or addressed, you do not adapt to the change and your stress will remain. The body will continue to react as if it is under threat and there is a high risk of developing long-term illnesses as natural resources become depleted over time.

These illnesses range from high blood pressure and heart attacks to psychological disorders, such as anxiety and depression. So it is very important to learn new techniques which, when the stress response kicks in, will aid in bringing your body back to a state of equilibrium.

So, now you know what the stress response is and why you may react in a certain way when under pressure (fight or flight). But what happens when the stress response doesn't get rid of your problem? We indicated that it is less effective with the pressures you encounter regularly as opposed to the life and death scenarios which it was originally intended for, so how do you get your body back into a state of equilibrium? The Stress Model below outlines the stages of the stress response and also highlights the stage at which you can intervene with new techniques and methods of thinking to combat the effects of the stress response.

The Stress Model

Alongside the stress response or physiological effects of stress, you also encounter a number of psychological (thoughts, images and feelings) and behavioural responses (how we behave) when you are under pressure. Figure 1.1 illustrates how the stress response can fail to remove the stress faced in today's pressurised environment.

FIGURE 1.1
The Stress Model (Palmer and Strickland, 1996)

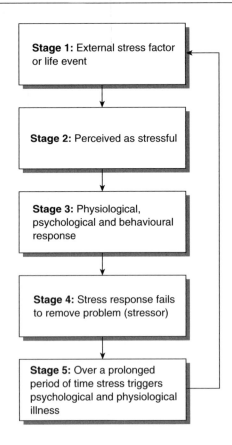

At **Stage 1**, the problem occurs, for example forgetting your house keys. However, as mentioned earlier, a situation only becomes stressful once we *perceive* it as being so, and this occurs in **Stage 2** of the model, so, for example, realising that you are locked out of the house as a result of not having your keys and deciding that this situation is stressful.

Stage 3 occurs almost immediately after you have perceived the situation or event as stressful. Our body and mind begins to react or respond to the stress. This happens in three ways:

1. Physiological response – these are the physical changes that happen in the body which you can usually identify, such as a thumping heart, sweaty palms, butterflies in the stomach or quick, shallow breathing.
2. Psychological response – these include the thoughts that may go through your head (*'Oh no, I can't believe this is happening to me!'*), and images or pictures of an event going badly. The negative emotions are also a psychological response and include anger, anxiety, guilt and embarrassment or, with long-term stress, depression.
3. Behavioural response – this is the way you behave in the stressful situation. This may include clenching your fists, pacing up and down, avoidance and procrastination and ritualistic behaviour (such as checking your pockets again and again for the keys).

If you have ever experienced being locked out of your home, you will know that none of the physiological, psychological or behavioural responses outlined above actually help you to get back into the house!

This leads us to **Stage 4** of the model – the stress response fails to remove the problem. The interventions that were used, such as getting angry or obsessive key checking, are not effective in removing the problem, and it is likely that your stress will remain. Unfortunately, until the problem is dealt with, such as finding your key, or another member of your household arriving home, your body may remain in a state of high alert if you still perceive the situation as threatening or stressful. It is only when the problem is dealt with or you put the situation into perspective that your body will go back to a state of relaxed equilibrium.

However, what happens if the problem is not as simplistic as the example above? Many of us have long-term situations or problems that may not have a straightforward answer (e.g. relationship problems, financial issues or workload pressures), which means that stress is sustained over long durations of time. Unfortunately, these continuous pressures can lead to dangerous levels of stress and the harm this can cause your body cannot be over-emphasised.

It is **Stage 5** of the model which highlights the potential hazards of being under stress for long periods of time or not tackling stress levels effectively. Stage 5 may involve more serious physical or psychological disorders or illnesses, such as ulcers or clinical depression.

If new techniques of dealing with stress are not found for long-term problems, your body will remain in a constant state of high alert. This cannot continue indefinitely.

Over time, your body's natural resources will deplete and this is when psychological and physiological illnesses may occur.

The techniques outlined in this handbook aim to tackle your stress levels at Stages 1–4 of the model. They may even help people in Stage 5 too but by then most people will need additional help from qualified health practitioners. We cover a range of techniques and interventions that have been designed to deal with the different types of stress that we encounter in a more effective manner. Using the example described above, a number of possible interventions can be used to reduce stress levels:

✓ The physiological response can be dealt with by relaxation exercises (e.g. taking deep breathes to slow down your heart rate) or self-hypnosis. This is covered in more detail in Chapter 4 and in Appendix 1.

✓ The psychological response can involve modifying the negative thoughts or reducing feelings of anxiety. More realistic thinking can relieve the stress, such as, *'okay the situation isn't great, but I can handle it'*. By reappraising the situation in a constructive and helpful manner, you are more likely to reduce your levels of stress. This type of thinking is dealt with in Chapter 3.

✓ A good behavioural response is to take a brisk walk round the block, to clear your head so you can think about how to deal with the situation more effectively. Exercise is a fantastic way of relieving pressure and helping us to think more clearly. Maintaining a healthy body and mind when under pressure is detailed in Chapter 8.

There are plenty of other techniques that can be used in addition to the ones illustrated above. By the time you reach the end of the handbook we hope you will have a repertoire of intervention techniques to assist you with any stressful scenarios you may face at university, work or in your social life.

Case study The Stress Model

Amy is a first-year business studies student. The following case study illustrates the different ways Amy reacts to the course requirement of doing a presentation. The stages of the stress response are illustrated throughout the example.

Amy was enjoying her undergraduate business studies course until her tutor mentioned the one task she was dreading – the assessed presentation dates! Amy had been given three weeks to prepare for the assignment, which she would then present to fellow students. There would also be time allocated at the end of her 15-minute talk for questions.

Stage 1 – The presentation is the external factor

Amy had a presentation to give to her tutor group at university.

Stage 2 – Amy perceives the presentation as a stressor

Amy was petrified:

'I would do an additional 10 pieces of course work just to get out of this! I am going to look like such an idiot in front of my class – I just can't do this', she thought. (*Appraised the situation as threatening*)

Stage 3 – Physiological, psychological and behavioural stress response comes into play

For the first week, Amy moaned about the presentation to all her friends (behavioural response). However, by the middle of the second week, Amy began to get very anxious. Although she had an idea of what she was going to present, she had done little preparation. She was too busy worrying about all the ways her presentation could go wrong! *'I must try harder'*. (*Psychological response*)

As the date came closer, Amy found she started having difficulty sleeping; she was beginning to eat less as she felt sick every time she thought of the presentation! She had even stopped moaning to her friends, as just the mention of the presentation would get her heart thumping and her hands would become cold and clammy! *(All physiological responses)*

Amy had also noticed that she had started biting her nails again and was going through nearly a packet of cigarettes a day, which was much more than she normally smoked *(behavioural responses)*.

By the beginning of the third week, Amy was running out of time. All Amy kept thinking to herself was, *'I just can't do this, I just can't' (psychological response)*. Out of desperation she decided to negotiate with her tutor. She asked to do an alternative to the presentation, such as an additional piece of course work. Her tutor was not impressed and explained that presentation skills were a key part of the course. There were no alternatives; she would have to do the presentation. Amy argued with the tutor *(behavioural response)*, but in vain, as neither the date changed nor the fact that she would have to do the presentation. She thought, *'No one understands my situation. It's so unfair.'* Understandably she felt out of control *(psychological response)*.

The night before the presentation, Amy stayed awake all night preparing. She knew the topic area very well, but would get nervous when she tried to practise the presentation *(psychological response)*. She began to imagine just standing in front of the tutorial group not being able to say a word *(psychological response)*. By morning, Amy was exhausted – she did not feel prepared and decided that she would not turn up for the presentation. She asked a friend from her group to inform the tutor that she was ill.

Amy felt better for a few hours, but then started to think, *'I'm stupid for not giving it my best shot'*. Most people would have been nervous today. She thought of her tutorial group – everyone would know she lied and the tutor would be annoyed with her too. She became angry with herself, *'I should have done the presentation'*.

Stage 4 – Stress response fails to remove the causal factor

The next day, Amy received a letter from her tutor informing her of a new date for her presentation. She had two weeks and again it would be performed in front of the tutor group – the difference was that she would be doing it alone. Everyone else had completed their presentation the previous day.

On realising this, Amy burst out crying. All her anxieties about doing the presentation came flooding back and in addition she felt a heightened sense of fear. There was no way of getting out of this. She had to get it done and she only had two weeks to prepare! This was added pressure and her previous approach to dealing with the problem did not make it go away. *(All the body's responses – physiological, psychological and behavioural – reappear to a greater extent)*.

If she wanted to avoid **Stage 5** of our stress model from occurring, she would need to prepare and give the presentation.

What the case study above shows us is that the body's automatic reaction to stress is not effective for all situations. As Amy's presentation date got closer she began to display symptoms of the stress response.

Her **physiological symptoms** included: sleeping difficulties, reduced appetite, feelings of nausea, tiredness, palpitations (throbbing heart) and crying.

Her **psychological symptoms** included: negative attitudes or thinking, such as an *'I just can't'* mindset. Holding this rigid belief convinces Amy that she is unable to carry out the task at hand. Other psychological symptoms included anxiety, anger, fear, feeling out of control, nervousness, worrying, feelings of helplessness and vivid catastrophic images (e.g. standing in front of the tutor group and not being able to say a word). Again this negative imagery would reinforce her belief that she is unable to do the presentation.

Her **behavioural symptoms** included: moaning to her friends, procrastinating or avoiding the task of preparing the presentation, biting her nails, smoking excessively, arguing with her tutor and avoidance of the tutor group.

Yet none of these behaviours assisted Amy in effectively doing her presentation. Furthermore, the case study illustrates that when an individual flees (procrastinates over the presentation) or fights (argues with the lecturer), it is unlikely that either of the two responses will remove the stressor (doing the presentation). Unless Amy tackles elements or areas that she perceives to be stressful about the presentation she will not only maintain but also possibly increase her levels of stress over the next two weeks. As she has not confronted her fears she is unlikely to be more effective than she was the first time she attempted to do her assignment, and the compounded stress levels may surge to greater and more daunting heights.

How could a situation like Amy's be effectively dealt with?

Let's look at her unhelpful belief. Amy believes that she '*just can't do*' the presentation. Where has she got the evidence for this? Has she attempted to give a presentation before or spent years avoiding speaking up in class? How does she know it's impossible? Other students give presentations. Her negative thinking is undermining her. It could even become a self-fulfilling prophecy! The views that she places on herself are likely to heighten her levels of stress by making her feel more anxious.

Amy can reduce her levels of stress by modifying her thinking. She can make it more realistic, constructive and helpful. For example:

'*It may not be fun but I can get through this presentation. If I make a mistake, it does not mean I am stupid. It just shows that I need to work on my presentation skills – with more practice I will improve.*'

If Amy chooses to use this coping statement and starts to focus on preparing for the presentation, she increases her chances of success. Although it may seem like a simplistic change, the power of words is often forgotten. How you phrase a thought can have a big impact on both your perception of an issue and how you behave towards the problem. Recall that Amy said, '*I must try harder*'. To illustrate the power of words and beliefs, do this small exercise in your head.

We will look at how the way we express our thoughts impacts on our stress levels in more detail in Chapter 3.

Coming back to Amy's behaviour, we notice that she avoids doing the task for the first two weeks; she is busy moaning and not really facing the problem. Had Amy

Have a go! Coping strategies

Close your eyes and imagine:
Trying to push a boulder off a cliff.
Try really hard.
Once you have visualised this, open your eyes.

DON'T look below until this exercise is completed ...

Close your eyes again and now imagine **pushing** a boulder off a cliff.
Just **push** it over.
Once you have visualised this, open your eyes.

What was easier? Did you find that you were not able to push the boulder off the cliff the first time round? Or if you did, was it harder to do than when you attempted it the second time round?

Another quick example is to **try** and clap your hands **now!**
What did you do?
If you clapped your hands, then you didn't do what we asked
    you to do!
When you **try**, your hands would not have touched**.**

Often the word **try** is an attitude of mind that denotes effort but **not** action. So if you want to get a task completed, **don't try ... just do!**

gone to her tutor at an earlier stage, she may have been able to get some useful tips on how to do the presentation and the tutor is likely to have been more sympathetic to her concerns. However, her reaction was not uncommon. Avoidance or procrastination is behaviour that many of us may resort to when we are uncertain or uncomfortable about tackling a problem.

Assertion techniques would have given Amy more confidence to tackle her fear of presentations as well as helping her to approach her tutor for help in a more constructive fashion. Amy would also benefit from time management skills to assist her in preparing her work earlier on. Procrastinating only served to escalate her stress levels in the last week prior to the presentation.

Instead of having vivid catastrophic images, including standing in front of the tutor group and not being able to say a word, every day before the event she should have practised seeing herself coping with the presentation – seeing herself standing up in front of the group and giving an adequate presentation and attempting to answer questions.

Amy also had a number of physiological responses, such as palpitations, difficulties sleeping and biting her nails. The best ways of dealing with physiological responses of stress is to expel that nervous tension which has built up in the body either by relaxing or by exercising. Both techniques have been found to reduce anxiety and depression, assist in anger management and act as distraction from problems by relaxing the mind. So either technique is likely to assist Amy by putting the situation into perspective and calming her down.

Although it may be easy to spot where Amy went wrong in dealing with her fear of presentations, it is not always that easy to identify stress-inducing thoughts and behaviours in yourself. Yet, without knowing how you react when you are feeling stressed, you are less likely to recognise the warning signals that your body sends you in the initial stages. The following exercise is designed to increase your awareness of your own reactions to stress.

Have a go! Reacting to stress

Everyone reacts to stress differently. Therefore it is important for you to understand your own pattern of thinking, your behaviour and your physical reactions to stress. Look at the lists below and tick the symptoms you experienced the last time you were under stress.

How do you know when you are stressed?

Psychological effects = How you think, picture and feel

- Anxious
- Angry
- Depressed
- Frightened, nervous or apprehensive
- Guilty
- Hurt

- Jealous
- Obsessive
- Ashamed or embarrassed
- Tense
- Drained, no enthusiasm
- Cynical
- Helpless

(Continued)

(Continued)

- Reduced self-esteem
- Increased worrying
- Lack of concentration
- Mood swings
- Withdrawal into daydreams
- Intrusive thoughts or images
- Nightmares
- Suicidal feelings
- Paranoid thinking

Physiological effects = how your body reacts

- Palpitations, throbbing heart
- Pain and tightness in the chest
- Indigestion
- Breathlessness
- Nausea
- Muscle twitches
- Tiredness
- Vague aches and pains
- Skin irritation or rashes
- Increased susceptibility to allergies
- Tendency to clench fists or jaw
- Fainting
- Frequent colds, flu or other infections
- Constipation or diarrhoea
- Rapid weight gain or loss
- Alteration of the menstrual pattern
- Cystitis or thrush
- Asthma
- Backache or neck ache
- Excessive sweating
- Migraines

Behavioural effects = how you behave

- Prone to accidents
- Poor work
- Increased smoking
- Aggressive or passive behaviour
- Irritability
- Impaired speech
- Increased absence from college, university or work
- Sulking
- Increased alcohol consumption
- Clenched fists
- Checking rituals
- Compulsive behaviour
- Talking, walking, eating fast
- Change in sleep pattern
- Loss of interest in sex
- Withdrawal from supportive relationships
- Overeating or loss of appetite
- Anorexia, bulimia or bingeing
- Poor time management
- Early morning waking
- Increased caffeine intake

Were you surprised at the number of ways you might react? It is important to check which responses you feel first when under excessive pressure as that is our body's way of alerting us. Once we are aware of our own reactions, we should be in a better position to address the symptoms and deal with the problems we are facing more effectively.

Chapter summary

This introductory chapter has given you a brief outline of what stress is and how the body reacts when under strain and stress. We hope that this chapter has enabled you to:

✓ Understand the definition of stress

✓ Identify the physiological, psychological and behavioural reactions to stress

✓ Recognise your own reactions to stress

✓ Establish the nature of your own reactions to pressure and your vulnerability to the negative effects of stress

At the end of each chapter, there is a space for you to write down any thoughts you may have relating to what has been covered. It is recommended that you use this space to write down any problems that you want to deal with and any useful strategies that were mentioned in the chapter which you feel may assist you in managing your stress. In Chapter 18 there is a stress action plan where you can identify the techniques and strategies that you have found useful. These can then be incorporated into a plan of action to deal with the stresses of university that you want to overcome.

Learning points from the chapter

Helpful resources

Centre for Stress Management

156 Westcombe Hill, London SE3 7DH

Tel: 020 8853 1122

Website: www.managingstress.com

Provides stress counselling, coaching and training services and undertakes stress audits and interventions at work.

***Conquer Your Stress*. Cooper, C. and Palmer, S. (2000). London: Chartered Institute of Personnel and Development.**

A stress management handbook that equips the reader with skills and techniques to help them handle the stress in their everyday lives.

2

What about your stress levels?

What this chapter covers
This chapter will look at your stress levels. It is quite a hands-on chapter with questionnaires and exercises for you to complete. The aim is for you to gain a greater understanding of what your stress threshold is and to identify what factors influence your ability to cope. In particular we will be looking at the differences between pressure and stress, how much control you perceive you have over your environment and what your personality traits are.

We all have different thresholds for stress and some react better in the face of adversity than others. However, there are many factors which influence our ability to cope with stress. For example, at different stages in our life we tend to find that our ability to deal with difficult or trying situations change, probably because our priorities and outlook may alter over time. Furthermore, our stress levels are mainly influenced by our own perceptions of a situation. Some of them are quite obvious, such as our perceptions about the amount of work we have to do, whilst others are slightly more subtle, such as the amount of control we perceive we have over a certain situation, or the values and beliefs that we hold about the way things should be done. In addition, our own personality traits play a big role in how we encounter stress.

Pressure versus stress

We all need a certain level of pressure to feel appropriately challenged, as this motivates us to complete tasks efficiently. However, pressure begins to turn into stress when an individual no longer perceives that they can cope with the situation they are in.

Figure 2.1 illustrates the relationship between pressure and the ability to cope. Everyone needs the right amount of pressure to perform at their peak. However, what this peak is will differ from person to person.

Where are you on the graph? Do you need more, or less pressure to be working at your optimum performance level? It is useful to keep a copy of the graph on your wall and check where you would position yourself on it each week. The graph is a good indication of how well you are coping with university life at any particular

FIGURE 2.1

The relationship between pressure and the ability to cope (adapted from Palmer and Strickland, 1996)

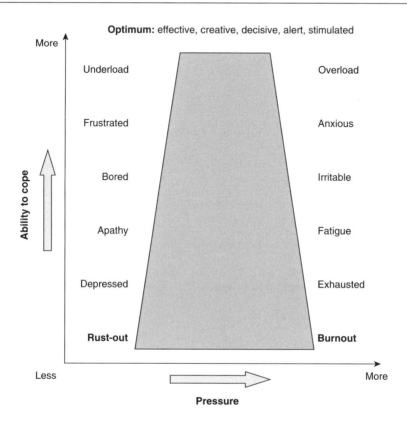

moment in time. Don't forget that too little pressure can be just as stressful as too much pressure, which is a fact that isn't often mentioned.

If you find that you are not performing at your peak, you may be finding situations more stressful as opposed to more pressurised. So, how effective are your current methods of coping with stressful scenarios? If you are unsure, the following questionnaire may help, as it looks at how you handle situations which cause you stress and how effective and helpful your behaviours are in dealing with the problems.

The life stress questionnaire (adapted Cooper et al., 1988)

Think of a problem you are finding difficult to deal with and which is triggering stress. It can be anything from adjusting to university life, to problems with family, friends or partners.

Temporary Adaptation – Part 1	Never	Rarely	Periodically	Regularly	Very often
Get on with work, keep busy	1	2	3	4	5
Throw yourself into work	1	2	3	4	5
Do some housework	1	2	3	4	5
Try to do something where you don't use your mind	1	2	3	4	5
Cry on your own	1	2	3	4	5
Bottle it up for a time, then break down	1	2	3	4	5
Explosive, mostly temper, not tears	1	2	3	4	5
Treat yourself to something e.g. clothes or a meal out	1	2	3	4	5

Helpful behaviour – Part 2	Never	Rarely	Periodically	Regularly	Very often
Sit and think	1	2	3	4	5
Ability to cry with friends	1	2	3	4	5
Get angry with people or things which are causing the problem	1	2	3	4	5
Let feelings out, talk to close friends	1	2	3	4	5
Talk things over with lots of friends	1	2	3	4	5
Go over the problem again and again in your mind and try to understand it	1	2	3	4	5
Feel you learn something from every distress	1	2	3	4	5
Talk to someone who can do something about the problem	1	2	3	4	5
Try to get sympathy and understanding from someone	1	2	3	4	5

Unhelpful behaviour – Part 3	Never	Rarely	Periodically	Regularly	Very often
Try not to think about it	5	4	3	2	1
Go quiet	5	4	3	2	1
Go on as if nothing happened	5	4	3	2	1
Keep feelings to yourself	5	4	3	2	1
Avoid being with people	5	4	3	2	1
Show a 'brave face'	5	4	3	2	1
Worry constantly	5	4	3	2	1
Lose sleep	5	4	3	2	1
Don't eat	5	4	3	2	1
Control tears (hide feelings)	5	4	3	2	1
Eat more	5	4	3	2	1
Wish you could change what happened	5	4	3	2	1
Have fantasies or wishes about how things might have turned out	5	4	3	2	1

Unhelpful		*Helpful*
29	87	145

When you think of the situation, to what extent do you do the activities listed in the questionnaire opposite? Ring the number that most accurately reflects your reaction.

Calculate your score by adding up all the circled numbers. If you have a score less than **58** it would appear that many of your behaviours to deal with stress are not always very helpful, whilst a score of a **116** or over would indicate that your behaviours are conducive to dealing with stressful situations.

If you find that your overall score appears to be quite low, identify which behaviours or thoughts you scored low on. In particular, focus on actions that will help you to raise the scores in parts 2 and 3 of the questionnaire. Note down the items that you would like to change. Consider how you may go about taking a different approach to dealing with stress-provoking problems. Even if you got a relatively high score, you may still want to improve on it.

As you go through the handbook, you will find techniques to assist you in dealing with stressful circumstances. These techniques will also highlight ways of changing any unhelpful behaviours which you may display when confronted with stress. Once you have familiarised yourself with other approaches you will be able to re-visit the answers given in this questionnaire and replace unhelpful behaviours and thoughts with a more positive approach.

Some of the answers you gave in the questionnaire could also be explained by your personality. People with certain traits are likely to respond to stressful situations in a particular way. The next section looks at the Type A and Type B behaviours and how they impact on stress levels.

What's your style?

Friedman and Rosenman (1964) came up with the labels 'Type A' and 'Type B' behaviour to describe specific behaviour patterns they noticed with their patients. Since then, these labels have been used by numerous psychologists under different guises to explain coping patterns, learnt styles of behaviour and personality traits.

Research has indicated that people who display Type A behaviour and characteristics are more prone to stress and may have an increased risk of suffering from coronary heart disease (Rosenman et al., 1975).

The main **Type A** behaviours identified include:

- A chronic sense of time urgency
- Impatience
- Rapid speech and aggressiveness
- Very competitive

Type A people are also often high achievers and extremely competitive (would you play to beat a child at chess for a piece of chocolate?).

In direct contrast to these behaviours, **Type B** individuals are described as being

- Easy going
- Patient
- More relaxed
- Not competitive

On the whole they are viewed as having a much more laid-back approach to people and situations and it is also believed that they are less likely to suffer from coronary heart disease.

Complete the questionnaire to find out what type of behaviour you exhibit.

What type are you – A or B?

Circle one number for each of the statements in the questionnaire on page 27 which best reflects the way you behave in your everyday life. For example if you are generally always on time for lectures, for the first statement you would circle a number between 7 and 11. Whilst if, on the other hand, you are usually very laid back about attending lectures on time, circle a lower number on the scale, between 1 and 5.

How Type A are you? If you have a greater tendency towards Type A behaviour, it is important to remember that Type A behaviours tend to trigger stress, frustration and anger responses. To deal effectively with this you may need to focus on how to reduce these stress-inducing characteristics. A number of ways of dealing with Type A behaviour is dealt with in later chapters of the book, including assertiveness training, anger management, relaxation and time management skills.

In addition, you are likely to hold a number of innate beliefs or values about how the world around you functions. Whether you feel you have a control over issues affecting you or whether you feel your life is not in your hands, the views you hold will impact on your level of stress.

Are you in control?

The term **locus of control** is used to indicate the amount of perceived control an individual believes they have in a given situation. If an individual attributes control to external forces and situations (e.g. *'it is fate!'*), they are said to have an **external locus of control**. An individual with an **internal locus of control** believes they have control and influence over the situation (e.g. *'I am not going to let this happen – I am going to sort this out!'*).

Research indicates that if you feel that you are in control of your life, that is you have an internal locus of control, you are less likely to suffer from stress. The reasoning behind this is that you will be more proactive in changing a stressful situation or more

Type A behaviour

Casual about appointments	1 2 3 4 5 6 7 8 9 10 11	Never late
Not competitive	1 2 3 4 5 6 7 8 9 10 11	Very competitive
Good listener	1 2 3 4 5 6 7 8 9 10 11	Anticipates what others are going to say (nods, attempts to finish for them)
Never feels rushed (even under pressure)	1 2 3 4 5 6 7 8 9 10 11	Always rushed
Can wait patiently	1 2 3 4 5 6 7 8 9 10 11	Impatient whilst waiting
Take things one at a time	1 2 3 4 5 6 7 8 9 10 11	Tries to do many things at once, thinks about what to do next
Slow deliberate talker	1 2 3 4 5 6 7 8 9 10 11	Emphatic in speech fast and forceful
Cares about satisfying him/herself no matter what others may think	1 2 3 4 5 6 7 8 9 10 11	Wants good job recognised by others
Slow doing things	1 2 3 4 5 6 7 8 9 10 11	Fast (eating, walking)
Easy going	1 2 3 4 5 6 7 8 9 10 11	Hard driving (pushing yourself and others)
Expresses feelings	1 2 3 4 5 6 7 8 9 10 11	Hides feelings
Many outside interests	1 2 3 4 5 6 7 8 9 10 11	Few interests outside work/home
Unambitious	1 2 3 4 5 6 7 8 9 10 11	Ambitious
Casual	1 2 3 4 5 6 7 8 9 10 11	Eager to get things done

```
         Type B                                    Type A
           14                  84                    154

            |_____|_____|
```

Source: Cooper et al., 1988 (Type A Scale), adapted from Bortner's Type A Scale (Bortner, 1969)
To find out your score, add up all the circled numbers above and mark it on the grid below to find out your personality type.

confident in your ability to do something about the problem, this in turn will reduce your anxiety or stress. However, if you have an external locus of control, you are more likely to feel that there is little that you can do about the problem you are facing, which in turn will make you feel more helpless or depressed, which will increase your levels of anxiety. Assess whether you have an internal or external locus of control by using the questionnaire on how much control you have, see page 28.

How much control do you have?

Circle the number that best reflects your attitudes.

	Strongly disagree	Disagree	Uncertain	Agree	Strongly agree
Our society is run by a few people with enormous power and there is not much the ordinary person can do about it	1	2	3	4	5
One's success is determined by 'being in the right place at the right time'	1	2	3	4	5
There will always be industrial relations disputes no matter how hard people try to prevent them or the extent to which they try to take an active role in union activities	1	2	3	4	5
Politicians are inherently self-interested and inflexible. It is impossible to change the course of politics	1	2	3	4	5
What happens in life is pre-destined	1	2	3	4	5
People are inherently lazy, so there is no point in spending too much time in changing them	1	2	3	4	5
I do not see a direct connection between the way and how hard I work, and the assessments of my performance that others arrive at	1	2	3	4	5
Leadership qualities are primarily inherited	1	2	3	4	5
I am fairly certain that luck and chance play a crucial role in life	1	2	3	4	5
Even though some people try to control events by taking part in political and social affairs, in reality most of us are subject to forces we can neither comprehend nor control	1	2	3	4	5

To find out your score, add up all the circled numbers above and mark it on the grid below.

Internal		*External*
10	30	50

Being too high on either extremes can trigger anxiety, although leaning towards a more internal locus of control is likely to reduce your stress levels on a day-to-day basis.

Although research does indicate that it is preferable to have an internal locus of control, it has been found that if you are internally focused, when situations are totally out of your control, such as freak weather conditions or train delays, you are more likely to feel anxious and stressed than an individual who has an external locus of control. This is because of the discomfort you feel by being out of control and unable to change the situation. So, there are benefits to both types of thinking, the idea is to aim for a balance between the two.

Chapter summary

This chapter illustrated the differences between pressure and stress, and gave you a practical insight into how you currently deal with stress. It also looked at your Type A behaviour and your perceptions of how much control you have over your immediate environment. Three questionnaires were used in this chapter. These were:

✓ The life stress questionnaire

✓ Type A or Type B questionnaire

✓ Locus of control questionnaire

By using the questionnaires in this chapter, you would have been able to identify styles of behaviour which are not conducive to dealing with stress, as well as ones which are. As you go through the handbook you will find a number of effective techniques for dealing with unhelpful approaches to handling stress. Having identified ways in which you react, you are more likely to find a technique that is suitable for you. It may be useful to note down any particular behaviours that you identified in yourself which are unhelpful for reducing your stress levels. Use the space provided below.

Learning points from the chapter

Helpful resources

International Stress Management Association
PO Box 348, Waltham Cross EN8 8XL
Tel: 07000 780430
Website: www.isma.org.uk

Provides information about stress management and accredits members.

British Association of Behavioural and Cognitive Psychotherapies
The Globe Centre, PO Box 9, Accrington BB5 0BX
Tel: 01254 875277
Fax: 01254 239114
email: babcp@babcp.com
Website: www.babcp.org

Provides a list of accredited therapists who deal with stress, anxiety, phobias, panic attacks and depression using cognitive-behaviour therapies.

Part 2   How can you handle your stress?

No matter how many precautions and preventative steps you take, difficulties and problems do arise. In spite of this, you can still be prepared for these encounters by learning to expect the unexpected. Furthermore, when you are aware of an impending stressful situation, you can learn to equip yourself with skills to handle the situation that you are concerned about.

In Part 2, we will cover a number of techniques to help you deal more effectively with stress-provoking problems. The techniques are generic to any stressful situation and are not limited to the context of this book. However, as with any problem-solving technique, practice is required to benefit from the skills that are outlined. The main techniques which are covered include:

- Thinking skills
- Imagery and relaxation
- Assertion and anger management skills

Each of the chapters in this part will introduce you to a new method or technique to deal with stress and they are complemented with case studies and examples to explain the methods in an easy and user-friendly fashion. You may find it easier to use some techniques rather than others, and this is due to personal style and preference. Make use of whatever you feel comfortable with.

By the time you have finished reading Part 2 of this handbook, you will be equipped with a skill set which can be applied in a variety of stressful scenarios.

3
Thinking skills

What this chapter covers
This chapter explores how your thoughts can impact on your stress levels. It includes a model of stress which can help you to break down your thought processes, to show where negative or unhelpful thinking can increase stress levels. It also highlights thinking errors that you may make when exposed to uncomfortable levels of pressure. In addition, the chapter includes information on realistic thinking skills which assist you in reducing anxiety when you are faced with stressful scenarios.

It's in the way we think!

Over the years psychologists have tried to understand what triggers stress among individuals and a variety of explanations have been given. However, for the purpose of the handbook we will focus on the cognitive approach, which has been gaining popularity among psychologists over the last 50 years.

The cognitive approach suggests that stress is caused by **thoughts** and **beliefs** that we hold about a given situation, as opposed to the situation itself.

Let's take the act of doing a bungee jump. There are some students who would be excited at the prospect of jumping off a bridge with only a rope attached to their body. It would give them *such a buzz*. Then there are other students who could not think of anything more stressful than hurling themselves off a bridge. *Why would anyone do that to their body?*

The situation in both instances is the same, a bungee jump. Yet what is different is the perception or thoughts that the student holds about it, and this defines whether it is stressful or exciting.

Your thoughts determine what you as an individual find stressful, and what you are able to cope with.

Thinking your way back to positivity

The way you think has a great impact on the way you handle problems when you are under pressure. In a stressful situation you are likely to find it harder to keep a positive frame of mind, which in turn restricts your effectiveness in problem solving.

In this section we will illustrate a new way of thinking and how to combat the downwards spiral of negativity when we become stressed. The six-step approach outlined below shows that the way you think is the key factor in the way you perceive the world around you.

The six-step approach (adapted from Ellis, 1977)

1. **A**ctivating event or situation – This is the situation/problem which we are concerned about, for example having to do a presentation in front of a tutor group.
2. **B**eliefs – These are the beliefs we hold about the situation, for example, *'I am too nervous so I can't do this presentation'*, *'everyone is going laugh at me and I can't stand that!'*
3. **C**onsequences – These are the automatic responses which occur due to the thoughts and beliefs that we hold. This is the result of the stress response, for example emotional responses such as being tearful and anxious, physiological responses such as butterflies in the stomach, a thumping heart whenever the presentation is mentioned, behavioural responses such as withdrawing from friends and becoming quiet, being snappy and irritable.
4. **D** = Disputing the negative beliefs – For example, *'will everyone laugh at me?'*, *'Am I being realistic?', Can I do something to reduce my anxiety so I can do the presentation?'*
5. **E** = Effective new approach to deal with the activating event at step 1, such as learning new relaxation skills or understanding what aspects of doing the presentation causes the anxiety.
6. **F** = Staying focused on your goals – Use the learning process involved in achieving your effective new approach to enhance your future performance.

By using this approach we are able to analyse any stressful situation.

Example 1

Think back to a time you had to do an important essay or assignment and you felt under pressure. What types of thought hindered you from performing effectively during that period?

- *Did you believe that: I do not have enough time?*
- *Did you believe that: I do not have the correct information?*
- *Did you believe that: I have too many other things that need to be done now?*

How did these ideas make you feel?

- *Depressed?*
- *Anxious?*
- *Nauseous?*

What thoughts and beliefs would have been more helpful in this situation?

- *I haven't got time to get more information, let me just do the best with what I've got*
- *If I prioritise my work I will be more effective*
- *I won't have time if I keep worrying about it. Once I start I'll be okay*

The case study below illustrates the types of thought that went through Michael's head when he had a deadline for an important piece of course work. Note how the different stages of the approach outlined above assist in the way he thinks.

Activation event or situation A	Beliefs B	Consequences C	Disputing these beliefs (B) D	Effective new approach to deal with the activating event E	Focus F
Unable to start writing an essay.	I must have all the facts/ information before I begin.	Anxiety	Must I? Who says I do?	Decide which areas are the most important and concentrate on making sure I answer the question, rather than telling the lecturer everything I know about the topic!	If I stop being a rigid perfectionist, I will be more effective in essay writing.
			Is it realistic to think I could get **all** the information available on the topic?		
			If I search too many sources I will probably end up with too much information!		
	I don't have enough time to get it done.	Depressed and frustrated	I can *make* time and prioritise my tasks for the day to ensure that I have time to concentrate on this assignment.	Stop procrastinating! Make a list of the things to do and prioritise them in order of importance.	

(Continued)

(Continued)

Activation event or situation A	Beliefs B	Consequences C	Disputing these beliefs (B) D	Effective new approach to deal with the activating event E	Focus F
	I should have started it earlier – there is no way I can get it done in the time allocated!	Palpitations	If I don't finish the assignment on time, it won't look good but it won't be the end of the world. Anyway, it's more likely to be late if I don't start it now!	Stay focused on the task at hand. Keep saying to myself *'just do it!'* for motivation.	
	It's such a difficult subject area – I don't know where to start!	Difficulty sleeping	I'm having difficulty starting the essay. If I write the main argument of the essay, when I come back to the beginning it will be easier.	Make a skeleton structure so I can see the points I want to make before I start. Practise my relaxation techniques when I am feeling anxious and before going to bed.	

Have a go! The six-step approach to thinking your way back to positivity

Think of a problem that you are stressed or worried about, or have been worried about recently **(A)**. Think of the beliefs that you held about the problem **(B)** and how these thoughts affected you **(C)**.

Challenge these thoughts **(D)** by coming up with more realistic or positive ways of dealing with the situation **(E)**. Remind yourself of why you want to overcome the problem and stay focused on how you deal with the situation so that you are effective in any similar situation in the future **(F)**.

(Continued)

(Continued)

Activation event or situation A	Beliefs B	Consequences C	Disputing these beliefs (B) D	Effective new approach to deal with the activating event E	Focus F

As illustrated in the section above, when you start thinking negatively you begin to feel stressed and this in turn hinders your ability to tackle the problem effectively. The next section highlights the different types of negative thinking you may be prone to and how these thoughts can be challenged.

Negative and unconstructive thinking

It never rains, but it pours. (Unknown)

When you feel under stress, you naturally become more negative about your ability to deal with the situations that arise around you. Psychologists have come up with a number of **thinking errors** that frequently hinder our problem-solving abilities when in stressful situations. Some of these are outlined below:

- **Focusing on the negative** – Instead of looking at events and situations in perspective, you only focus on the negative:
  'It's raining on my barbeque party! It's all going wrong!'
  A more helpful way of thinking may be:
  'Shame about the rain! However, everyone appears to be having a great time indoors, even if the food's coming from the oven!'

- **Discounting the positive** – Anything positive you discount as luck or unimportant:
  'I can't believe I got picked for the football team – someone must have pulled out last minute!'
  A more realistic thought could be:
  'My coach appears to have noticed an improvement in my playing skills. All my practice is paying off!'

- **Mind reading** – You assume that people are reacting to you in a negative way when there is insufficient evidence that this is the case:
  'I just got blanked by someone I met yesterday – they obviously didn't think much of me.!
  An alternative and more realistic thought would be:
  'It's pretty crowded here, they may not have noticed me.'

- **Fortune telling** – You predict the worse case scenario, often with insufficient evidence:
  'It's my 18th birthday next week. I bet the DJ will turn out to be crap!'
  Rather than thinking of nothing but doom and gloom on a day you are excited about, use the facts presented to you:
  'I saw the DJ at a gig last week and he was really good, so he should be just as good at my party!'

- **Magnification or awfulising** – You blow events out of proportion and make mountains out of molehills:
  'I just flunked my first-year economics exam. This is really awful. I think I should just give up now.'
  Although failing any exams can be quite a knock to your self-esteem, it is more helpful to look at where you may have gone wrong:

'Luckily, this was my first-year exam so I have plenty of time to improve. The result is bad but hardly awful. I will look at sample papers and see how I can improve my revision and exam techniques.'

- **Emotional reasoning** – You evaluate situations by how you feel:
  'I feel hurt, so I must have been treated badly.'
  It may be more helpful to detach yourself from the situation slightly:
  'Maybe I am being too sensitive. I should try to see this from their perspective too.'

- **Blame** – Instead of taking any personal responsibility you blame others for problems that might have occurred:
  'Who moved my book? I am sure it was here yesterday!'
  A more helpful way of approaching this may be:
  'Let me think back to the last time I saw the book, let me retrace my steps ...'

- **Demands on self** – This occurs when you hold unrealistic expectations or rigid beliefs about the way you should behave or deal with a given situation. These are usually expressed as *'shoulds'*, *'musts'*, *'got to's'*, *'have to's'* and *'ought to's'*:
  'I must pass the exam' or *'I must make a good impression'*.
  When you are already in a stressful situation, do you really need the added pressure of high expectations on yourself? Although it would be desirable for these outcomes to happen, there is no law in the world that says *you have to* have the outcome you expect. Stating a preference is less demanding of yourself and is a much more effective way of thinking when you have to focus on the task at hand:
  'I really want to pass these exams and I have prepared well for it. That is all I can do. It's pointless winding myself up!'

- **Phoney-ism** – You fear that others may find out that you are not the person you portray yourself as being:
  'Oh no! When they ask questions after my presentation they are going to realise that I don't really know what I am talking about!'
  Is this really true? How often have you thought that way about someone else doing a presentation? A more helpful way of thinking could be:
  'If I can do a presentation on this area, I know the topic well enough! If I can't answer a question, I can always get back with an answer later.'

- **I can't stand it!** – You lower your tolerance for dealing with adversity or frustrating situations by telling yourself that *'I can't stand it'* or *'I can't bear it'*:
  I have to get out of the traffic jam – I can't stand it!'
  Is this really true? You have been *standing it* until now. It would be more helpful to accept the situation and attempt to take your mind off the stressful thoughts:
  'Although I do not like traffic jams, I'm living proof that I've stood them before! So rather than focusing on how frustrating it is, I can put on the radio and enjoy the music.'

Have you been able to recognise any of these thinking errors in the way you deal with a given situation?

Have a go! Types of negative thinking

Use the space provided below to write down examples of when you have used these types of negative thinking. Or add thinking errors that you regularly make which are not on the list.

Focusing on the negative:

Discounting the positive:

Mind reading:

Fortune telling:

Magnification or awfulising:

Emotional reasoning:

Blame:

Demands on self:

Phoney-ism:

I can't stand it!:

Any other thinking errors:

It is easy to fall into the trap of negative, unhelpful thinking but how can you change certain views and beliefs that you hold to gain a more positive, constructive and helpful thought process? Now that you have completed the thinking error exercise, we can introduce some methods to help you to modify some of those beliefs.

Realistic thinking

Accept that some days you're the pigeon, and some days you're the statue. (Roger C. Anderson)

When things go wrong it is very easy for you to lose perspective, label the whole day as being *bad* due to the negative experience or even begin to believe that nothing ever goes right! These types of thinking not only hinder your ability to solve problems effectively, but also cause tension, keeping you in a *worked up* state. As shown earlier, the way you think can directly impact on the way you behave and feel. Therefore, the more you begin to view situations in a positive and realistic light, or see the silver lining in a cloud, the more likely you are to feel calmer and, as a result, be more effective in dealing with difficult situations or problems.

Interestingly, we tend to find it easier to think of the negatives of a situation as opposed to searching out more positive ways of confronting a difficult scenario. Below are some thinking skills to assist you in putting negative thoughts into perspective. They are not there to dispel the problem as being unimportant, but to assist you in being more realistic in approaching it.

Befriend yourself – Think about how you would treat a friend or family member who finds themselves in a similar situation to you. Would you be as harsh on them as you are on yourself?

De-labelling – Substitute extreme and emotive language with beliefs that are less evocative. For example, if you describe yourself or a fellow student as being '*a complete waste of space*' or a '*total failure*', examine the idea more closely. If someone really was useless or a waste of space, how did they manage to get into university?

Think relatively – If you think in extreme terms (i.e. something is either perfect or rubbish), try to see some middle ground to ensure that you maintain a level of perspective.

'*Even though I do not have the time to ensure the grammar of my course work is perfect, I do have the time to take a number of steps to minimise the number of errors which could be present in the essay.*'

A pros and cons list – List all the advantages and disadvantages of the behaviours, thoughts or emotions being held when under stress. See the table below.

State behaviour and/or thought and/or emotion: *Going to the Freshers party on my own*

Pros	Cons
• *I am likely to blend in as everyone is in the same boat*	• *I will look like I have no friends*
• *Gives me a great opportunity to meet new people*	• *I might have to stand around for a while on my own*
• *I can see what others are wearing before going into the Student Union*	• *I might embarrass myself if I'm not wearing the right type of clothes*
• *I get to check out the party scene here*	
• *I haven't got any plans for this evening*	
• *Although I prefer not to go to the fresher party on my own, I am sure lots of other students are feeling the same*	
• *I can leave early if I am not enjoying myself*	

© 2005, Centre for Coaching

Have a go! Pros and cons of beliefs and ideas when under stress

Think of a problem that you are currently attempting to resolve. Fill in a pros and cons table to help you to brainstorm the arguments *for* and *against* the belief or thoughts you hold about the problem. Sometimes it can be difficult to think of a more positive approach when you are so closely involved in it. If this is the case, you may find it helpful to ask friends and family for their ideas.

State behaviour and/or thought and/or emotion:	
Pros	**Cons**

Test assumptions – If you believe that you cannot handle a particular situation, push yourself to test the assumption. For example, if you find it stressful to stand in a crowded bar for more than 10 minutes, test the assumption by pushing yourself and standing in the bar for 15 minutes. By doing this you are learning to stand *outside the box* which you have created and challenge your beliefs directly.

Talk to others – We often assume that our problems are unique and that no one else could possibly understand what we are experiencing. Ask people whom you trust about your problem. You may be surprised to note how many people have been in a similar situation or feel the same way as you!

Demagnify or 'deawfulise' – Whatever the situation, if you blow it out of proportion, you are very likely to increase your stress levels. Of course certain events may be very difficult to deal with, but are they really the *'end of the world'*, the *'worst day of your life'*? Seldom are the events that we face on a day-to-day basis really that bad.

Broaden the picture – When things go wrong you may find yourself blaming yourself for the events that have occurred (personalisation) or blaming other innocent parties, such as a partner, friends or lecturers. However, problems are rarely caused entirely by just one person – the responsibility is likely to lie with a few individuals or circumstances.

A useful technique to deal with this is to write down all the people or issues you feel are involved in the problem and distribute the blame proportionately. This can be represented in a pie chart. This will enable you to illustrate everyone's part in the situation and the amount of responsibility to assign to them, as well as the amount to assign for yourself. It is rare that one person is totally to blame.

Case study Thinking realistically

Situation: Chris failed his first-year economics paper. He blames himself entirely for not working hard enough. However, on reflection, once he had broadened the picture, he realised he was not completely to blame, and there were other factors, which had contributed to the situation. (See bottom pie chart.)

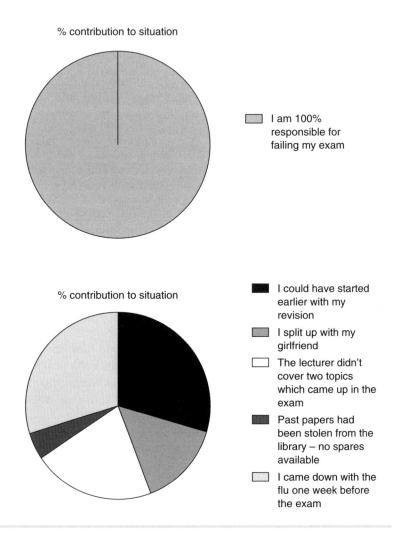

% contribution to situation

I am 100% responsible for failing my exam

% contribution to situation

I could have started earlier with my revision

I split up with my girlfriend

The lecturer didn't cover two topics which came up in the exam

Past papers had been stolen from the library – no spares available

I came down with the flu one week before the exam

So the next time you find yourself becoming agitated and worked up, remember your thinking skills to help you keep things in perspective!

Chapter summary

This chapter covered a number of techniques which can be used to identify and replace negative and unhelpful thinking with more helpful and stress-reducing beliefs. The chapter included:

✓ The six-step approach – this model helped to identify and analyse how you think when you are under pressure

✓ Negative thinking – this highlighted a number of thinking errors you may make when you are stressed and which hinder your ability to problem solve effectively. This included errors such as blame and mind-reading.

✓ Realistic thinking – this illustrated ways of disputing the negative thoughts which may arise when you are stressed. The techniques included befriending yourself, creating a pros and cons list and thinking relatively

Learning points from the chapter

Use the space provided below to write down any thoughts or comments you have about this chapter.

Helpful resources

Association for Coaching

66 Church Road, London W7 1LB
Email: enquiries@associationforcoaching.com
Website: www.associationforcoaching.com

Holds a register of coaches.

United Kingdom Council for Psychotherapy
167–169 Great Portland Street, London W1W 5PF
Tel: 020 7436 3002
Fax: 020 7436 3013
Email: ukcp@psychotherpy.org.uk
Website: www.psychotherapy.org.uk

Holds a register of psychotherapists.

Life Coaching: A Cognitive-Behavioural Approach.
Neenan, M. and Dryden, W. (2003). Hove:
Brunner-Routledge.
This book shows how to tackle self-defeating thinking and
replace it with a problem-solving outlook.

4

Imagery and relaxation skills

What this chapter covers

This chapter addresses two methods of dealing with stress. Section 1 covers imagery, which is a proactive technique that addresses the visual images individuals may have about a stressful or anxiety-provoking situation which is yet to occur or which is currently impacting on you. The four main types of imagery covered in this section include: coping imagery, time projection imagery, motivation imagery and relaxation imagery.

In section 2, we explore how relaxation can assist in reducing your stress levels. The techniques outlined in the section include: diaphragmatic breathing, meditation and easy-to-use, stress-busting techniques.

Section 1: Imagery

Imagery is a powerful method of stress reduction, especially if you visualise your thoughts and feelings about situations in pictures and mental images inside your head. When you are stressed or worried about a situation you are more likely to conjure up negative mental images of the event or situation going wrong. These images are likely to increase your anxiety and stress levels.

'I had a lecturer who would go through your work during the lecture in front of everyone else. It was mortifying! I dreaded going to her lectures – I'd always imagine her as being this big giant, glaring down at me, waiting for me to make that one mistake, so she could enjoy her moment of glory. I would picture her picking me up in her big hand and showing me to the rest of the class as being an example of stupidity! A bit extreme I know, but she really did intimidate me that much!'

Michael, 22 years, Aberdeen

As Michael's images illustrate, the mental picture does not have to be realistic, but it can still provoke anxiety. Michael found the lecturer so intimidating that he soon conjured up negative images of her and how she dealt with him. Having negative images can be very stressful, and as time goes on they are likely to make it harder for you to handle the problem effectively. In fact you may choose to avoid the situation completely.

Have a go! Imagery

Think of the last time you were really stressed or worried about a future event. Picture the event in your head. Do your negative images invoke greater feelings of stress or do they calm you down?

Fortunately, there are a number of imagery exercises that have been designed to alleviate some of the stress you may encounter by negative images. This section will focus on a number of imagery exercises that have been found to be beneficial in reducing the negative images you may sometimes experience under stressful circumstances. These include:

- Coping imagery
- Time projection imagery
- Motivation imagery
- Relaxation imagery

Coping imagery

This technique enables you to edit the image in your mind by replacing the negative and stressful scenario with a more helpful yet realistic interpretation of a situation.

Notice that this type of imagery is called *coping* and not *mastering* imagery. This is because if you are concerned about your ability to handle a situation it is unlikely that you will be comfortable imagining yourself handling a situation perfectly – as it will probably feel unrealistic. Coping imagery helps an individual to accept that they may not be able to give the perfect presentation or be the life and soul of a party but if things go wrong, they are equipped with the skills to deal with the problem.

The technique consists of four simple steps:

Step 1 – Think of a future situation that you are stressed about.

Step 2 – Note down the aspects of the situation that you are most stressed about.

Step 3 – Develop ways to deal with these difficulties.

Step 4 – Practise the new approaches to dealing with the difficult situations

Practise step 4 daily, especially when you become stressed about the forthcoming event.

This simple approach can be used for a wide range of problems. For example, if you are stressed about being asked difficult questions after giving a presentation, then you need to focus on how you would deal with this situation if it did actually occur. Don't pretend that it might not happen. Perhaps you might decide the best strategy would be to inform the audience that you are unsure of the answer to that particular question but will get back to that person after the presentation. This strategy would then become the key aspect of the visualisation that would be practised in step 4.

Case study Coping imagery

Bob is an 18 year-old student. He has wanted to ask Stacey from his tutor group out on a date. He has been told that she is going to be at the Student Union on Friday night. Although Bob is very eager to ask her out, he is very anxious that she will say no and he'll look stupid in front of his friends.

Bob keeps imagining Stacey saying no and sometimes visualises her laughing in his face. But his worst fear is his friends watching him when Stacey tells him that she is not interested.

Bob developed a new picture to deal with this potentially stressful scenario – Stacey rejecting him. Instead of standing around awkwardly and getting embarrassed, which was his current mental image, he imagined himself casually walking away from Stacey towards his friends and shrugging his shoulders. This was much more acceptable and less anxiety- provoking than his previous image, as he felt he still maintained a level of dignity in the process.

Bob practised the new image every day. Although the picture varied sometimes from him shrugging his shoulders and walking away, to him shrugging his shoulders and saying to his mates *'Oh well, it was worth a go! You win some, you lose some!'*

The anxiety of asking Stacey out was reduced as he had learnt a new way of dealing with the worst possible outcome he could imagine!

Although this may appear to be a simple technique, many people get stuck at step 3, as they are unable to develop ways to deal with the situation. In these cases, it may help to discuss the problem with a colleague or friend. Remember, the idea is to deal with your worst fears and not to pretend that they simply may not happen. This method helps to prevent negative images becoming self-fulfilling prophecies, by challenging and addressing negative thoughts and images.

Time projection imagery

So often, people lose their perspective when they are faced with stressful situations such as failing an exam or breaking up with a partner. Time projection imagery helps you to keep stressful situations in perspective by assisting you to realise that the problem or situation may not be *that bad.*

Method

Step 1 – Think of a problem or situation that you are stressed about.

Step 2 – Picture yourself three months in the future. Will the current problem be as stressful as it is now?

Step 3 – Picture yourself six months in the future. Will the problem be as stressful or as important as it is now? Can you see yourself getting on with your life?

Step 4 – Picture yourself 12 months in the future. Will the current problem be as stressful or as important as it is now? Can you see yourself getting on with your life?

Step 5 – Picture yourself two years in the future. Will the current problem be as stressful or as important as it is now? Will you laugh at your problem when you look back on it? Can you see yourself having fun again?

Are you getting the idea? The technique is all about taking a step back and looking at the problem afresh.

Case study **Time Projection imagery**

Lisa received her exam results for a module that she had been struggling with all year. She had failed the exam by 5 per cent and was devastated. Lisa had persevered with the course even though she found it difficult. Failing the course made her question her ability and she felt that all her hard work had gone to waste.

Lisa used time projection imagery to help her put the examination result into perspective.

She pictured herself in three months time. Was the result still stressful? Lisa felt it wouldn't be as intense as it was now, but it would still be a worry for her. She would need to decide whether she was going to retake the module or just accept her mark which would impact on her pass mark for the year.

Lisa then imagined herself thinking about the exam result in six months time. Was it still as important and stressful? Lisa felt that she wouldn't be as worried after such a long duration. She would have decided whether to retake the module or not by then, and would probably be taking a course of action to rectify the situation. However, she thought she would still question her abilities to a certain extent.

Lisa pictured herself 12 months into the future. She imagined that she would have moved on by then. She would be into her next year at university and this mark would have no relevance to her anymore. She believed that she would take on board the lessons learnt from this experience but it would not impact on the way she lived her life in any other way!

By doing the time projection imagery, Lisa was able to establish how much relevance and importance to place on the exam result. Although she had to deal with the problems it raised in the immediate future, its long-term implications appeared to be minimal.

Motivation imagery

This technique is used to motivate people into action and can be applied to any given situation or problem (Palmer and Neenan, 1998). The technique highlights the impact of doing nothing compared to seeing your goals through.

Have a go! Motivation imagery

Think about an area of your life that you need to do something about. Until now you may have avoided thinking about it or have found you are too busy to change the situation. For example, starting a piece of course work or finishing a relationship that is no longer working out.

Now imagine you do not do it. What impact is this likely to have on you? Would you have any regrets if the situation stays the same? How do you feel about it? Happy or sad? How do you think the people around you may react?

(Continued)

(Continued)

Now imagine making the change (i.e. starting the course work or splitting up with your partner). What would be the short-term, medium-term and long-term benefits that the change would make in your life?

Finally consider how you are now going to make that change. Put your thoughts into action.

Please note that the order of the exercise should stay the same, beginning with imagining that you do **not** change the situation and then imagining that you do act and change the situation. Only then can it aid your motivation to carry out the task. Doing it in the reverse order can be demotivating!

Relaxation imagery

When you are feeling stressed out, imagery is a fantastic tool to unwind, releasing all the tensions of the day. The aim of relaxation imagery is to help you to imagine yourself relaxing in a place which gives you comfort and or that you enjoy being in. This then leads to you actually feeling more calm and relaxed. This technique has been found to be very useful for people who suffer from sleeping problems. To use this imagery, just follow the nine simple steps outlined below (Palmer and Strickland, 1996):

1. Find a place where there is as little noise as possible, and where you will not be disturbed.
2. Either lie or sit in a comfortable position.
3. Close your eyes and picture your favourite relaxing place.
4. Concentrate on the colours in this place.
5. Concentrate on one particular colour.
6. Concentrate on the sounds in your place. It may even be complete silence.
7. Imagine touching something in your place.
8. Concentrate on the smells and aromas in your favourite relaxing place.
9. When you are ready, open your eyes.

You may find it easier to record your voice or have someone read this out to you for the first few times. After a while you will find that you automatically follow the steps and will be able to reach a relaxed state quickly and without much effort. You can make it last only a few minutes or extend the exercise for up to 20 minutes.

Section 2: Relaxation techniques

There are a number of different ways to relax and you are the best judge of what works best for you. Relaxation can range from painting, listening to music to meditation and positive relaxation imagery. The aim of relaxation is to re-energise yourself by giving your body and mind time to wind down and forget about the day-to-day issues it has to deal with. By clearing your mind of tensions whilst you relax, you are likely to find that when you re-visit a problem at a later stage, you will be able to deal with it more efficiently.

In this section, we will introduce you to a few different methods of relaxation, including deep breathing, meditation and easy and quick relaxation tips to use when you are on the go!

Breathing

Our chest is full of muscles which pull our ribs up and down as we inhale and exhale. This is what enables us to breathe. We need oxygen to work our muscles and so the air we inhale is passed through our lungs and into our bloodstream, from where the oxygen is passed around the body. How we breathe is a great indicator of how we are feeling. When we are nervous or anxious, our breath is shallow and fast, whereas when we are relaxed our breath tends to be slower and more controlled. There are many breathing techniques which assist in relaxation by slowing down our breath. In this section we will concentrate on diaphragmatic breathing.

Diaphragmatic breathing

Although this is not the natural way we breathe everyday, it is great for energising or relaxing our body and mind. Diaphragmatic breathing allows more oxygen into the body, by taking longer and deeper breaths. The technique is outlined below.

Step 1 – Gently fill your lungs up with air (your chest will naturally rise up and your stomach may come out slightly).

Step 2 – Gently breathe out through the nose (your chest will drop) and squeeze your stomach in to dispel all the carbon dioxide from the lungs.

Step 3 – Repeat the exercise two or three times, or until you feel less stressed and calmer.

This breathing technique gently massages the abdominal organs and makes you aware of how you breathe.

Please note: People who suffer from asthma, anxiety attacks or have smokers cough may have some problems with deep breathing. You may experience dizziness. Please do the breathing exercises gradually and only breathe in and out at a level which is comfortable for you.

Laughter

It may seem like just another cliché but we all know how great we feel once we have had a good laugh. It has been suggested that one minute of extensive laughter can provide up to 45 minutes of relaxation. Laughter is great for the body as it releases tension and stimulates the immune system. It is also said to create a feel-good factor by releasing endorphins into the blood.

A simple smile can have an impact on the way we feel. A smile is the universal expression of happiness, and apparently the most frequently used facial expression. Supposedly, even if you fake a smile, it can make you feel better!

In addition, people who are more relaxed are said to live longer, healthier lives and are better to cope able with pain. They are also meant to be able to handle difficult people more effectively too!

Massage

Massage is a brilliant way to relieve the tension and stresses of the day! The basic goal of massage is to help the body heal itself and to increase health and well-being.

Many practitioners learn specific techniques, in which they use their sense of touch to determine the right amount of pressure to apply to each person and also to locate where the areas of tension are.

When we are stressed, our muscles can become very tense and overworked. This produces waste products which can cause soreness, stiffness and even muscle spasms. By improving circulation, which increases blood flow and brings fresh oxygen to body tissues, massage assists in eliminating waste products from the body.

Therapeutic massage can be used to promote general well-being and enhance self-esteem, as well as boosting the circulatory and immune systems to benefit blood pressure, circulation, muscle tone, digestion, and skin tone. Massage is found in many different forms (such as Swedish massage, shiatsu or Indian head massage), so it is worth finding out what is available before embarking on a course of treatment. Also, self-massage can be a useful skill to learn as you do not need to rely on others.

Relaxation methods

Relaxation methods are techniques to progressively relax your body and calm your mind. Three relaxation methods are included in this handbook:

- Guided light meditation
- The Benson Relaxation Technique
- Self-hypnosis

The self-hypnosis method is available in Appendix 1 of this handbook. You may find that one strategy works better than the other so give them a go and see which one you prefer.

These relaxation methods are written out as scripts below. You may find it useful to ask a friend to read them out to you or record your own voice reading them and play it back whenever required. During the relaxation exercises you may experience tingling or a warm sensation. This is quite normal. However, if you do not like it, gently open your eyes and the sensation will stop.

Guided light meditation

Guided light meditation uses more imagery than other types of meditation. The aim is to imagine moving the light from a candle to different parts of your body. Whilst you do this, you automatically become more relaxed. However, if you find it hard to visualise the light, you may find the mantra meditation more suitable (the Benson Relaxation Technique).

This exercise requires you to light a candle and place it carefully in a safe place, at a sensible distance away from the body (a few metres away from the body). The candle should be placed at your eye level. Sit comfortably on the floor or on a chair. (The script is to be spoken out loud.)

Gently lower your shoulders and relax the body. Forget about all the things you have been doing today, and all the things you still have to do. Be present, in this room, now *(pause for 5 seconds)*

Feel the air in the room gently brush against your face …

(Continued)

(Continued)

Listen to the noises inside the room *(pause for 5 seconds)* ... now take your hearing outside this room, take it as far as it can go *(pause for 5 seconds)*

Now bring your hearing back into the room ... and look at the candle flame in front of you.

Look carefully at the flame – notice its colours and the aura around it *(pause for 10 seconds)*

Gently close your eyes and **imagine** taking the light from the candle flame to your forehead, between your eyebrows ... and into your head. Let your head fill up with light from the candle *(pause for 10 seconds)*

Now imagine moving the light behind the eyes and let the eyes be filled with light *(pause for 5 seconds)*

Now imagine the warmth and light of the flame move into you ears ... now move it to your mouth and tongue *(pause for 5 seconds)*

Now imagine the light gently travelling down your arms ... to the hands ... right down to the fingertips ... and let the light permeate them *(pause for 5 seconds)*

Allow the light to gently move down through the body ... imagine it slowly moving down the legs ... to the feet and right down to the toes *(pause for 10 seconds)*

Now gently bring the light back to the head *(pause for 5 seconds)*

Expand the light ... let it become brighter and brighter *(pause for 5 seconds)*

As the light fills your body ... let it then radiate the room ... let the light fill the room with brightness *(pause for 10 seconds)*

Now staying with that calmness, bring your thoughts back into the room you are sitting in *(pause for 5 seconds)*

Become aware of your feet and body ... notice the air gently brush against your cheeks ... hear the noises in the room *(pause for 5 seconds)*

Remember what you still have to do today ... and remember throughout the week that if you want to relax all you have to do is fall still, as you have done so now.

Slowly count to 10 ... and when you feel ready, gently open your eyes.

The Benson Relaxation Technique

The main difference between the Benson Relaxation Technique (Benson, 1976) and the guided light meditation is that one visualises light going through your body and the other concentrates on repeating the number 'one' or another number of your choice. It is down to personal preference as to which one you find easier to do.

Find a comfortable position in a place where you will not be disturbed. (The script is to be said out loud.)

Close your eyes

Relax your muscles in groups, starting at your face and progressing down to your toes *(pause for 10 seconds)*

Now focus on your breathing. Breathe naturally through your nose. Imagine that your breathing is coming from your stomach; do not let your shoulders rise *(pause for 5 seconds)*

In your mind, say the number 'one' every time you breathe out

(continue this for 5–20 minutes – finish when you feel ready, but keep still for a few minutes before opening your eyes)

Self-hypnosis

Self-hypnosis works by aiding you to relax and as you relax you become more receptive to positive or helpful statements made. Please note that self-hypnosis is not a form of controlling another person's senses or mind.

The self-hypnosis script can be found in Appendix 1.

Fitting relaxation into your life

When life gets hectic, we often find that our well-intentioned plans get left behind, as daily pressures build up. Time to *fit in* relaxation is less likely to happen if it is not planned, so you need to make the time for relaxation.

Have a go! Relaxation

Think about the scheduled activities that you have to do this week, including lectures, meeting family or friends, personal study time and so on. Based on the commitments you already have planned for the week, when can you fit in time for relaxation? It is easy to think of relaxation as being a bit self-indulgent, but if you want to be more efficient and effective in other aspects of your life, looking after your body and mind will help to keep those stress levels down!

Quick fixes

Stress can happen at any time! Unfortunately, depending on where and what you are doing, you may not always be able to use the relaxation techniques outlined in this chapter instantly. For those unexpected moments, we have a few quick fixes to help you out until you have more time to fit relaxation back into your life!

- Tap the centre of your chest rhythmically using the fingers of one hand – one heavy tap should be followed by two lighter taps (ONE, two, three; ONE, two, three). Do this for about two minutes.
- Place your elbows on your desk and put your face into your hands, cupping the palms over the eyes so the face is gently supported. Relax your shoulders and let go of any tension that you may be holding in your body. Even ten seconds like this is likely to make a difference.
- Give your shoulders a real exaggerated shrug. Once you have done this, tilt your head back as far as it will go, inhaling as you do so. Then gently exhale and release any tension. Let everything go. Your shoulders need to drop down as well. Concentrate on the heat in the back of the neck and shoulders as the blood there starts to flow freely again.
- Put a few drops of orange or lavender essential oil on a tissue. Inhale throughout the day or whenever you find yourself becoming anxious or stressed.
- Squeeze a stress ball (these are available from health or beauty shops). The simple action of squeezing reduces stress and massages a number of acupressure points.
- Smile for a minute! A smile is said to increase the production of serotonin, the happy hormone.
- Do this ayurvedic technique for soothing the brain. For as long as possible, gently massage the point in the middle of the forehead (the place of your third eye), preferably using a little sesame oil applied in a very light circular movement.

- If you feel restless or tearful and are not sleeping well, use Belladonna, a homeopathic remedy which is available in most health shops.
- Put a few drops of Bach Rescue Remedy into any drink. It contains various flower essences which help in relaxing you. It is available in health shops and most chemists.

(adapted from *The Times*, Energy Plan, 2001)

Chapter summary

This chapter was broken down into two sections. Section 1 explored how imagery can help you deal with negative images that you may have visualised in your mind's eye, especially when you are under uncomfortable levels of pressure. Four types of imagery were discussed:

✓ Coping imagery: editing a negative image and replacing it with a more helpful and less stressful scenario

✓ Time projection imagery: taking a step back from the problem and putting it into perspective

✓ Motivation imagery: highlighting the impact of not changing a situation or problem compared to taking action, and addressing the issue at hand

✓ Relaxation imagery: imagining yourself in a familiar and comfortable place, which helps to relax your mind and release your tensions

Section 2 of this chapter concentrated on relaxation skills to assist in alleviating stress and tension from your body and mind. Techniques included:

✓ Breathing: exercises to help energise or relax your body and mind

✓ Laughter: how laughter releases tension in the body and stimulates the immune system, promoting relaxation

✓ Massage: the effects of massage on the immune system and your feeling of well-being

✓ Relaxation scripts: methods of progressive relaxation which gently relax the body and still the mind

✓ Fitting relaxation into your life: the need to make time for relaxation and quick tips on instant relaxation!

Learning points from the chapter

Use the space below to write down any techniques or comments that you have from reading this chapter.

Helpful resources

***30 Scripts for Relaxation, Imagery and Inner Healing*. Julie T. Lusk (1992). Duluth, MN: Whole Person Associates.**
The book incorporates scripts for relaxation, ranging from five minutes to 30 minutes. Each script states at the beginning how long it should take and gives a brief description as to what to expect from the practice.

***Stress Relief and Relaxation Techniques*. Lazarus, Judith (2000). Chicago, IL: Keats Publishing Inc.**
This guide helps readers dissolve stress, gain clarity and cultivate a more peaceful existence with relaxation and stress relief therapies, ranging from meditation to massage, biofeedback and journal-writing.

5

Assertion and anger management techniques

What this chapter covers
This chapter is divided into two sections. Section 1 looks at assertion techniques whilst section 2 looks at how to manage your anger levels.

In section 1, we will cover the four main behavioural styles that we use when dealing with situations (aggressive, passive, indirect and assertive). There is also a questionnaire to help you identify how assertive you are. A number of assertion techniques are also outlined to assist you in being more effective when dealing with confrontational or stressful situations.

Section 2 will look at the reasons why you get angry. It will concentrate on challenging the anger response, so you can deal with confrontational or stressful situations in a rational way, which is less damaging to your health. In addition, an anger de-activating exercise is included. This will help you to increase your awareness of what your anger triggers are, and how you can learn to address them.

Section 1: Being assertive
Acting assertively is a fantastic way of managing your stress levels. It enables you to express your needs directly and calmly without causing conflict or misunderstanding. It helps you to stand your ground and prevent others from wasting your valuable time.

How do you behave?

Researchers have identified four types of behaviour that people display: aggressive behaviour, passive behaviour, passive-aggressive behaviour (or indirect behaviour) and assertive behaviour. The main characteristics of the four behaviour types are outlined below, along with their effectiveness in stressful or pressurised situations.

Aggressive behaviour

Aggressive individuals tend to react to stressful situations with hostility or anger, regardless of whether or not they are provoked by others. Their bursts of anger may even make them feel temporarily in control or even superior to others around them. In addition, aggressive individuals believe that they are being assertive, but the way they stand up for their rights often violates the rights of others. Eventually this behaviour may cause conflict with others as they become resentful of the aggressive individual's behaviour.

The main problem with aggression as a behaviour style is that it can belittle and insult other people. It may also anger others or intimidate them. Typical aggressive behaviour is characterised by feelings of anger, power or agitation. Aggressive people tend to be *bullies*, with behaviours ranging from pointing, shouting, thumping fists, to picking on other people's vulnerabilities to make them feel more powerful and superior. Their language is characterised by phrases such as '*You should be/you must / don't act dumb / this is all your fault!*'

In the long term, if an aggressive style of behaviour is consistently used, an individual is likely to upset friends and colleagues, and may find that they are unable to influence others, leading to feelings of isolation and rejection. They may also lose the respect of others, which can impact on their own levels of self-esteem. All of these potential outcomes will increase levels of stress.

Passive behaviour (Unassertive behaviour)

Unassertive people are often denoted as being the *mug* or *push over* in a given situation. Individuals who display this type of behaviour are likely to allow others to walk all over them. This behaviour is particularly unhelpful because these individuals end up doing things for others or accepting situations that they are uncomfortable with. So, they may end up regretting doing the favour or resenting others for *putting them in it* (blaming others). The type of language used by passive individuals includes phrases such as '*Could I? … Would it be okay if I …? It's not important … It doesn't matter … Never mind … Sorry to bother you.*'

Passive behaviour is often characterised by feelings of guilt – people are unable to gratify the wishes of others. This occurs alongside suppressed anger for being taken advantage of. Their behaviour tends to be apologetic and they avoid confrontation at any cost. Passive individuals lack self-confidence and this is displayed in their physical behaviour, for example through downcast eyes, shrugs or hand wringing. Unassertive individuals tend to play the role of the victim. They usually blame or whinge about a particular situation without taking responsibility for themselves (i.e. they forget that they *do* have a choice!). Unfortunately this behaviour may also lower one's self-esteem, as the passive individual is more likely to view themselves as powerless and helpless with regards to their circumstances. They are likely to have a high external locus of control (mentioned in Chapter 2), as they view circumstances as happening to them, and are more likely to see themselves as being too helpless to deal with the situation. These feelings and perceptions of themselves are likely to increase stress and anxiety levels.

Passive-aggressive behaviour (or indirectly aggressive behaviour)

Individuals who fall into this category tend to display a mixture of both aggressive and passive behaviour. They are likely to be more manipulative with their requests and can be more defensive in their approach to situations. Individuals who display passive-aggressive behaviour tend to be more moody, more controlling of other people and may use emotional bribery to get their desired response.

Initially, passive-aggressive individuals can be quite influential. However, over time, other people become wary or confused by their behaviour because of the mixed signals they receive from them. Passive-aggressive individuals use these techniques to protect themselves by avoiding confrontation, as they fear they may be undermined. However, this behaviour also leads to a reduction in self-esteem and self-confidence.

Assertive behaviour

Assertive people avoid misunderstandings and actively reduce the possibility of being exploited. It is a useful behaviour pattern because it deals with interpersonal difficulties in a straightforward and constructive manner, which reduces resentment. An assertive person uses co-operative statements such as '*we could*', or '*I feel*'. Assertive individuals are adaptable and collaborative in style and approach. They tend to be good communicators, both verbally and behaviourally. Physical behaviours include good eye contact and being both relaxed and confident. They make others feel valued, respected and listened to, whilst remaining confident themselves, and possess an inner sense of power.

The benefits of assertive behaviour are that it gets quicker results and the individual is in a good position to seize opportunities when they arise. Assertive individuals are also more likely to develop honest relationships that are based on mutual respect. An assertive individual is also more likely to be confident and have higher self-esteem. They suffer less stress as they are calmer and perceive themselves as having more control over their problems.

How assertive are you?

Fill in the following questionnaire to see whether you display assertive behaviour in the situations outlined below. Circle the response which best describes how you would respond in each of the following scenarios.

CAN YOU:	Yes	No	Sometimes
Say no when a colleague or friend makes an unreasonable demand?	Y	N	S
Accept compliments easily?	Y	N	S
Admit easily to mistakes?	Y	N	S
Apologise when it is your fault?	Y	N	S
Ask for help from others?	Y	N	S
Listen to criticism about yourself?	Y	N	S
Speak up for yourself?	Y	N	S
Express your feelings appropriately?	Y	N	S
Avoid being exploited by others?	Y	N	S
DO YOU:			
Take responsibility for your behaviour?	Y	N	S
Accept the consequences of your decisions?	Y	N	S
Tell friends your true opinion?	Y	N	S
Tell your lecturer if you are dissatisfied with your assignment?	Y	N	S
Readily ask for clarification if you do not understand something?	Y	N	S

Add up all the circles in the Yes column.

If you have 12 or more responses in this column you display assertive behaviour on a regular basis.

If you circle between 8 and 12 in the Yes column you are reasonably assertive and may just need to focus on a few areas.

If you have less than 8-circled responses in the Yes column you are likely to exhibit aggressive, passive-aggressive or passive behaviours that may need more attention.

As mentioned earlier, the less assertive you are, the more likely it is that some of your stress is a direct result of your lack of assertion. For example, it is very difficult being a good time manager if you are unassertive!

Getting assertive

Acting assertively helps you to maintain your rights and gives you the confidence to do what is right for you. Below are a few techniques on how to get a message across assertively.

The three-step model

The three-step model can be applied in any situation, but especially if you are feeling intimidated or under pressure to comply with other people's demands. Using this model, you can make your point in an assertive manner without offending, becoming emotional and, more importantly, without drifting off the point you are making.

The three-step model begins by clarifying what the issues are and repeating back the points mentioned. This conveys that you have been listening to the other person and also avoids any misunderstandings.

Step 1 – Actively listen to what the other person is saying and repeat it back to demonstrate that you have heard and understood what they have said.

The second step consists of stating your opinions about the situation. It is at this stage that you explain your own thoughts and feelings.

Step 2 – Say what you think and feel (a good linking word to use between steps 1 and 2 is 'however').

In the final step of the model, you explain what you want the outcome of the situation to be. This needs to be clearly stated to avoid any misunderstandings.

Step 3 – Say what you want to happen (a good linking word to use between steps 2 and 3 is 'and').

For example:

Step 1 – *I know I said I would come home this weekend,*

Step 2 – ***However**, I have an assignment due in on Tuesday and I think it would be a good idea to work on it over the weekend*

Step 3 – ***And** I will be coming home next weekend instead.*

Broken record technique

This requires you to keep on stating your own opinion – and to keep on expressing your viewpoint in a consistent manner until your message is not ignored. The words do not have to be the same; it is the essence of the statement or belief which is important. This is a particularly useful technique when others are putting pressure on you to do something that you do not want to do or do not have time for.

Friend: *Come out tonight, you have the whole day to revise tomorrow!*

You: *I know that, but if I have a late night today I won't be able to concentrate.*

Friend: *Yeah, but we are all going out – c'mon! It's only one night. It won't make that much of a difference!*

You: *I wish! It will be to me. Have a great night and cheers for asking!*

De-fogging

This is when you find a person manipulating a situation and possibly using irrelevant facts to get the outcome they want. You need to clarify what the discussion is about and keep irrelevancies out of the dialogue.

Flat mate: *You always leave your dishes in the sink and it's not fair for the rest of us to keep tidying up after you!*

You: *During this term it's the second time I have left the dishes in the sink, and I'm sorry for doing that.*

Inquiry

This really puts the onus on the others to come up with a good explanation or reason for their negative statements about you. It encourages constructive and helpful feedback.

Lecturer: *Your essay missed the point.*

You: *In what way did it miss the point?*

Workable compromise

With this approach an agreement is reached in such a way that your self-respect is not affected.

Girlfriend: *You promised me that we'd go out to eat tonight.*

You: *I didn't realise that the football was on. How about we get a take away tonight and I'll take you out for dinner tomorrow? Would that be okay?*

Section 2: Managing your anger

Anger is an instinctive response to stress and danger, but as the dangers we face today are generally not life threatening, we usually do not require the aggressive behaviour that anger can trigger.

We all feel angry sometimes. It is a normal, usually healthy human emotion. Anger only becomes a problem when it starts getting out of control or is the first emotion we use to deal with any given situation. So, in itself, anger is not a bad thing, but problems arise if it is not managed in the right way.

Most people do not realise the long-term effects of ongoing anger. Anger can lead to a number of physical illnesses, notably coronary heart disease. But in addition, it has a large number of other side-effects – it consumes mental and physical energy, ruins your peace of mind, can negatively impact on relationships and can undermine your self-esteem. In extreme circumstances, anger can be an all-consuming emotion, clouding your mind of reasonable judgement. All of these effects have a major impact on your stress levels.

Understanding your anger

If you find that your anger is out of control and affecting your quality of life, you may benefit from looking at the way you handle your feelings when you are angry.

Anger is the emotion you experience when situations or circumstances in your world are not going according to *your* plans! It can be an adaptive response to threats to the way your world should operate. Anger can be a very powerful emotion as it allows you to fight and defend yourself when you are attacked. Aggression is another behavioural reaction to the stress response described in Chapter 1. When you get angry, your heart rate and blood pressure go up, as do the levels of the hormones adrenaline and, in particular, noradrenaline in your body.

To stay in control of excessive anger you need to learn how to express your feelings in a healthier way, so your annoyance or frustration is a more controlled response to the situation you are presented with. There are several techniques to handle your anger, many of which have been covered in the thinking skills and imagery chapters of the handbook (Chapters 3 and 4). These techniques have been adapted below to be more specific to anger management.

Challenge your beliefs

As mentioned previously, your thoughts are very powerful and play a very large role in the way you react to events. When you are feeling angry, find out what it is about the particular situation or person that is causing it. What are the thoughts that go through your head once you are aware that you are getting angry (the triggers)? Do you see an image of them which upsets or annoys you? Or do you have a particular belief that keeps going through your mind?

Once you are able to identify the thinking errors or negative images you can begin to concentrate on creating new, more constructive ways of approaching the problem, which will lower your levels of stress and anger.

Case study Anger management

Rick found that he was losing his patience with his girlfriend every few days, and that usually the anger he displayed was unwarranted. Rick decided to write down the thoughts that went through his head every time he felt his anger manifesting and noted down why he was getting angry.

Rick soon noticed a pattern. Every time they tidied up the flat, he would find that he couldn't find some of his personal belongings. Rick couldn't stand anyone touching his possessions and he would get furious at the thought that his girlfriend may have misplaced his important documents or his CDs.

Rick wrote down a list of more helpful beliefs he could say to himself to counter-attack the negative thoughts and images that would wind him up and eventually get him angry.

Anger activating	Anger de-activating
Why does she have to touch my things?	She wouldn't have to if I put them away myself.
She has no respect for what I say!	Although I think it is wrong that she touches my belongings, does she really disrespect me? She is only trying to keep the place clean.
I bet she is looking really smug now that I can't find anything!	Imagine her feeling a bit concerned about how upset I am.
I told her I would move it myself!	That was last week. Maybe she did not think I would do it.
She always misplaces my stuff!	Am I exaggerating the truth? If she moves my stuff she normally puts it in one place, and she usually finds things I've misplaced!
I told her to leave my papers alone!	She warned me that if they were sprawled across the breakfast table, she would move them, and I didn't listen.

(Continued)

(Continued)

Anger activating	Anger de-activating
Does she do it just to irritate me?	Maybe she feels that I keep my belongings out just to irritate her.
The place is already tidy – I don't know what her problem is!	She knows she can be a bit over the top. I will tell her that she is being a bit unreasonable when I have calmed down.
I can't stand it when people touch my things!	Maybe it would be less stressful to think that *'I'd prefer it if she didn't touch my stuff. However, when she does I don't like it but I can stand it.'*

Have a go! Anger management

Think of a situation or person (or both!) which you feel angry about. Note down the negative thoughts and/or images that you have, and then challenge them by creating constructive ways of dealing with the situation or person which is not so anger-provoking.

Anger activating	Anger de-activating

Other issues to consider when dealing with anger

- **Is it worth it?** Even if you are right to be *justifiably* angry and someone or something has done wrong by you, does it make you feel happy? You are consuming a lot of energy which could be used elsewhere in a more enjoyable way! After the situation has been rectified or the problem discussed, remaining angry is usually pointless, because it doesn't change your circumstances. You are not able to change the way another person thinks and behaves and, generally speaking, you do not have the right to. Sometimes it may be better to '*live and let live*'.
- **Use logic!** Being logical defeats anger, because if anger is unjustified, it quickly becomes irrational. Remind yourself that this isn't the *worst day of your life* and that the day just didn't go according to plan! If you attempt to rationalise your thinking and use logic each time you feel angry, you will probably get a more balanced perspective of the problem. This is the approach most people tend to take once they decide to calm down. However, using logic earlier can save a lot of time!
- **Maintain communication.** When anger consumes you, you're more likely to make assumptions and jump to conclusions without fully understanding the whole situation. Nothing is more unproductive than two people arguing about two completely different issues without realising it! If you find yourself in a heated discussion, take a deep breath, slow down and think before you speak! Remember to listen to the other person, as everyone has the right to his or her own opinion.
- **Stay calm.** We realise that this may be easier said than done, but taking a few deep breaths or leaving the room for a quick walk can give you enough time to collect your thoughts and put the situation back into perspective.
- **Get fit.** If you find that you are feeling very tense on a regular basis, exercise is a great way of reducing the tension and it also gives you some time away from everyday stresses. Relaxation exercises such as yoga, relaxation imagery and meditation can also help to release the build-up of tension in a controlled and healthy way.

Chapter summary

The aim of this chapter was to equip you with skills that would help you deal with confrontational or anger-provoking situations in a more effective manner. The two skill sets used were:

✓ Assertion skills – including a variety of thinking skills and imagery to help you become more effective when dealing with conflict

✓ Anger management – highlighting techniques to help you deal with your anger by exploring what triggers your anger response

The techniques mentioned in this chapter are generic and can be used in almost any context. However, the rest of the handbook focuses on how to deal with stress within the context of life at university.

Learning points from the chapter

Use the space provided below to write down any thoughts or comments you have about this chapter. Are the techniques helpful in reducing your stress levels?

Helpful resources

British Association of Anger Management
Tel: 0845 1300 286
Email: info@angermanage.co.uk
Website: www.baam.co.uk
Professional body of consultants, counsellors and trainers who offer individual support, workshops, seminars and bespoke packages to assist with anger management

British Association of Behavioural and Cognitive Psychotherapies
The Globe Centre, PO Box 9, Accrington BB5 0BX
Tel: 01254 875277
Fax: 01254 239114

Email: babcp@babcp.com
Website: www.babcp.org

Provides a list of accredited therapists who deal with stress,
anxiety, phobias, panic attacks and depression using
cognitive-behaviour therapies.

***Asserting Your Self*. Birch, C. (1999). Oxford: How to Books**
The book offers a variety of techniques to help transform
unhelpful defensive behaviours into productive and assertive
ways of being.

Part 3   Starting university life

Starting university is an exciting time. You will be meeting a variety of people from all walks of life and are likely to be exposed to a number of new experiences. But what happens when Freshers week finishes and the university routine begins?

In Part 3 of this handbook, we will cover some of the problems that may arise once the euphoria of being at university begins to wear off. Chapter 6 discusses the transition from leaving home and beginning university and the issues of feeling homesick and leaving friends and family behind.

Your living environment can also have a big impact on how quickly you adapt to university life. Chapter 7 looks at the different types of accommodation available to you and discusses potential problems that may arise when living with other students.

Eating what you want and when you want may well be a welcoming change when you join university. However, it is not long before take-away food loses its appeal and the craving for home-cooked food starts! Chapter 8 concentrates on ways to maintain a healthy regime without having to spend lots of money. It also looks at your lifestyle to assess how healthy you really are!

It is only when you begin your course that you can really know whether you chose the right one. In Chapter 9 we give tips and pointers on dealing with the stress of realising that your course does not meet your expectations.

Socially, it is at the beginning of university life that you will make the majority of your friends. This can be a particularly stressful time, as you need to introduce yourself to other people and may have to go to social events on your own initially. Chapter 10 includes advice and case studies to remind you that you are all in the same boat!

The final chapter in Part 3 addresses the issue of money! Your finances can be a very big stressor at university, especially as managing your money is imperative to ensuring that you have enough money to last you through the academic year! Chapter 11 includes information on how to budget and manage your finances in a simple and stress-free way!

University is said to make students more independent. This is usually because students are faced with responsibilities and situations that they probably never had to think about before. Although it can be said that this steep learning curve is a good experience, at the time it can be very stressful. We hope that the advice and techniques available in these chapters will help you to minimise the stress levels that can arise as you adjust to university life.

6

Leaving the nest

What this chapter covers

In this chapter we will briefly look at how leaving for university can impact on family dynamics and affect other relationships you currently have with friends and partners. Going to university is something to look forward to, but it can be stressful if the change is not managed adequately. This chapter addresses ways of maintaining contact with family and friends, and also looks at how to tackle homesickness.

On your way to university!

You did it! After all the hard work and effort you put into getting to university the time has finally arrived! There is a lot to be excited about – it's a new place, with new people and new challenges. However, as with all change and with any adventure, in order to move forward there are always some things you have to leave behind …

… the folks

This may well be the first time you are leaving home and it's likely that there is a part of you that's dying to finally have the freedom and autonomy to do what you want, when you want and where you want. However, you are also leaving the security of what you know, the comfort of your home and the familiarity of your surroundings. There is nothing wrong with feeling a little overwhelmed. Change can feel like a scary place.

In all the excitement, it is also easy to forget how the folks are feeling. It is a big transition for them as well. Whether they joke about it, *'finally we get the spare room we've always wanted'*, or lay on the emotional bit, *'I don't know how we are going to manage without you'*, it is possible that they are also going to find it a bit strange when you leave. Do keep in touch with them as it may give them some peace of mind.

... the friends

University enables you to meet a variety of different people from all walks of life and this will only help to expand your network of friends, rather than reduce it.

Although you may be anxious about losing touch with your friends, it is likely that they feel the same way as well. So don't forget to take their mobile numbers, email addresses and new contact details to keep in touch.

'Uni is a great place to make new friends but, personally, there is something special about friends that you've known for a long time – they understand you, warts and all! Even now, if I'm really excited about something or if I'm upset or feeling lonely, the first thing I'll do is call my best mate in London. The familiar voice is great to hear and she normally knows what to say to make me feel better!'

Nadia, 19 years, Bristol

... the partners

Leaving behind a loved one is hard, especially if they are not going to university. It's common to hide your excitement or to keep plans about nights out from your partners out of a sense of guilt.

'I'm sure she will feel bad if I talk to her about the party, especially as I had such a great time without her.'

Tom, 19 years, Leeds

It is never wise to make assumptions and an open and honest discussion with your partner about how your relationship may change whilst at university will be far more beneficial. Many couples find that university does not necessarily cause a break-up in relationships, especially if your partner is included in your future plans.

'I had been dating this guy for about six months before starting uni. It wasn't that serious so we agreed to see how things would develop. He was at a London university as well so it wasn't that difficult to meet up. But we made sure we did our own thing too. I think it worked out pretty well ... 10 years on and we are now married!'

Amber, 30 years, London

It is not unusual for students to be in a relationship when they join university. But whether a relationship lasts the course of university depends on the strength of your relationship, how you both handle the change and the emphasis you place on being together.

'Clare never went to university and wasn't really that happy when I got my place at Warwick. Once I started uni, we stayed in touch and met up, but as time went on we seemed to have less and less to talk about. I also felt that I was making all the effort to see her, as she never felt that comfortable coming to see me. I think we broke up three months into my first year. I did really like her ... but we both changed and had moved on.'

Jack, 23 years, Warwick

Starting university after completing your gap year

If you have just completed your gap year, leaving home may not cause as many anxieties for you, especially if you went travelling or stayed away from home during that period of time.

However, some gap-year students find it difficult to re-adjust to student life after their year out, feeling they have less in common with the other first-year students. Whether this is because you have been working in an office environment over the past year, or backpacking across Europe, it may feel like you have been experiencing a life that other students may not be able to relate to.

'I'm sure I alienated lots of people when I came back from travelling. Looking back I was really full of myself! I wanted to tell everyone about my adventures in India, Thailand and Australia, and to be honest, whatever they had to say about their summer after A Levels just paled into insignificance! I wasn't trying to be arrogant, I guess I was a bit immature, and I think I was still overwhelmed and excited about what I had actually done. I did eventually stop going on about my travels — but not until I noticed someone rolling their eyes when I said 'when I went travelling ...'

Paul, 21 years, Kingston

Although it is good to share your experiences and there is nothing wrong about being excited about your gap year, it is important to remember that not all first-year students have been in a similar position to yourself and may not share your enthusiasm, so try to limit the number of times you mention your year out, at least until you get to know your friends a bit better!

Some gap-year students also find that settling back after a year of not reading or even touching textbooks, can also cause them stress!

'I'd had one year where I barely wrote anything except the odd email and coming back to an environment where I sat in lectures and wrote notes was completely weird to me!

Marieke, 20 years, Portsmouth

Be prepared for the shock of putting pen to paper again! You may find it useful to get into a studying routine fairly early on. This will reduce the stress and anxiety when the assignments begin to come in, as you will be more prepared to deal with them.

Feeling homesick?

So you have been at university for a while now. The excitement of the freedom and independence might be wearing off a little. Are you fed up washing your own clothes and cleaning up after yourself? Are you missing home-cooked food? Your friends? Or have you just run out of money?

It is quite natural to miss home and adjusting to a new way of living does not happen overnight. It will take time and probably a few trips home to feel more settled.

Here are a few tips to help you along the way:

✓ Ensure that you have a regular method of contacting home which won't dip into your finances (possibly arrange a call card or a pay-as-you-go mobile phone which is used just to call home).

✓ Plan meetings. Arrange dates and times for meeting up with family and friends back home. This will help you to make sure that everyone is free to meet when you go back and gives you a date to look forward to.

✓ Learn a few of your favourite home-cooked recipes so you can make them during term time.

✓ Keep yourself busy. Initially, you may find it a bit of an effort to make friends and to join clubs and societies, yet it is very important to do so. Too much time on your hands can lead you to feel isolated and lonely.

✓ If you are feeling very homesick, it's worth making a trip back home. Many students find that they go home a bit more frequently in their first few terms than they do for the rest of their university years. However, if you find that you feel even worse after you make a trip home, you may benefit from making a conscious effort to stay at university and settle into a routine before going home again.

✓ Make your room feel like your own. Your room is probably very bare when you move in so decorate it in your own style. Display your favourite memorabilia and put up some posters and photos to make the room feel more personable to you. (Check the rules of your accommodation before putting things up on the walls.)

If you're finding it increasingly difficult to adapt to your new surroundings and are becoming depressed, you are not alone! This anxiety is not uncommon for many new students at university. However, if the symptoms of depression appear to be getting worse (such as complete fatigue, losing weight, tearfulness or feelings of hopelessness) and you do not feel you are able to cope, it is advisable to contact you local GP or your student counsellor.

Changes in relationship dynamics when you go to university

In some instances students find that they feel homesick because they are worried or concerned about friends and family back home. This leads to feelings of guilt or anxiety when at university. Whether you are worried about your partner being unable to cope with you being at university or your family falling apart when you leave, it is important to tackle the problem rather than feeing the unwarranted guilt.

Case study **Changing dynamics**

Ian had never lived away from home before moving to university. Although he was enjoying his first few weeks at university, he was very concerned about how his parents would manage without him. His parents had a rocky relationship and this was intensified by his mother's heavy reliance on alcohol. Ian had always been the mediator when they argued and without his presence, Ian was very worried about how they were coping. These thoughts kept him awake at night, and often made him think of packing up and going home.

Ian went home every weekend and called home everyday. However, he often found his mum crying down the phone. Ian was becoming depressed and anxious about what he could do.

Ian wrote down his stressful thoughts and then worked on how to think more positively about the situation. The SIT (stress-inducing thinking) and SAT (stress-alleviating thinking) form that Ian created is shown below.

PROBLEM: Leaving home	
Stress-inducing thinking (SIT)	**Stress-alleviating thinking (SAT)**
• *Mum and dad can't manage without me*	• *They managed before I was born and when I was younger*
• *I'm being selfish by enjoying myself at university, when they are so upset – I have a duty to look after them!*	• *They are both adults, and they both went to university – I would resent them both if I went home without completing my degree*
• *They may end up getting a divorce*	• *Although I would find that very difficult to cope with, it is their lives and if they are not happy why should I try to keep them together*
• *Mum is drinking more alcohol and it's my fault. She would be okay if I was at home*	• *Mum is making her own choices. I will go home this weekend and talk to her again about getting some help. But she shouldn't be that dependent on me. I will call her just once a week. I will be there to support her all the way, but I can't ruin my life just because she is adamant on ruining her own*
• *Things will change when I go back home*	• *I am already changing! I'm seeing my family in a new light and enjoying my own independence. I don't even know if I would want to go back to that environment again*

© Centre for Stress Management, 2005

Once Ian had clarified his thoughts he was able to tackle the problem more confidently. He discussed the form with his parents, explaining his concerns with them. He explained that he would only call home once a week, although his mother could call him on the mobile if she felt she really needed to. He also explained that he was there to support her if she decided to get help for her alcohol problem.

After the first month, which was very emotionally draining for Ian, things calmed down. His mother stopped calling him as often and was beginning to seek advice for her drinking with his father. When Ian went home over the Christmas holidays, he noticed that his parents had formed a stronger relationship whilst he was gone and they no longer relied on him to sort out their problems.

Ian admitted that he did feel slightly rejected that his importance was now diminished, but he knew they still loved him and he felt less guilty about living his own life at university.

Problems like Ian's are not uncommon. Leaving home can impact on the family dynamics in a number of different ways. If you are concerned about how things will change, you may find it useful to fill in the stress-inducing thinking/stress-alleviating thinking form below. This may help you to clarify your thoughts and can be a useful starting point to discuss your concerns with family or friends.

Have a go! Stress-inducing thoughts/stress-alleviating thoughts

If you are worried about how friends, partners or family members are going to cope without you at home. Or if you are concerned about how moving to university will impact on your relationships, you may find it useful to write down your concerns in the form below and dispute the stressful thought (SIT) with a more rational and helpful response (SAT).

(Continued)

(Continued)

PROBLEM:	
Stress-inducing thinking (SIT)	**Stress-alleviating thinking (SAT)**

© Centre for Stress Management, 2005

Chapter summary

This section deals with the transition from home to university. A few useful tips to help you acclimatise include:

✓ Good communication methods with family and friends back home

✓ Planning ahead

✓ Staying busy at university

✓ Adapting your university environment to make it as comfortable and homely as possible

✓ Confronting concerns about how university will change existing relationships and dynamics

Learning points from the chapter

Use the space below to write down any thoughts or comments you have about this chapter.

Helpful resources

The Site.Org

This website provides factsheets and articles on all the key issues you may face when starting university, including: sex and

relationships; drinking and drugs; work and study; housing; legal and finances problems; and health and well-being.
Weblink: www.thesite.org.uk/workandstudy/studychoices/whatcourse/thewrongcourse

Depression Alliance

Tel: 0845 123 2320 (all calls charged at the local rate)

Depression Alliance is a self-help organisation for people suffering from depression. It provides information, understanding and local self-help groups for the benefit of depression sufferers. Depression Alliance has three offices within the UK:

England

212 Spitfire Studios, 63–71 Collier Street, London N1 9BE
Email: information@depressionalliance.org

Wales

11 Plas Melin, Westbourne Road, Whitchurch, Cardiff CF14 2BT
Email: wales@depressionalliance.org

Scotland

Depression Alliance Scotland, 3 Grosvenor Gardens, Edinburgh EH12 5JU
Email: info@dascot.org

The Samaritans

The Upper Mill, Kingston Road, Ewell, Surrey KT17 2AF
If you are in crisis you can write to the Samaritans: Chris, PO Box 9090, Stirling FK8 2SA
Use this web address to locate the closest Samaritans branch to you: http://www.samaritans.org.uk/talk/local_branch.shtm

The Samaritans national helpline

UK: 08457 909090 (open 24-hours)
Republic of Ireland: 1850 609090 (open 24-hours)
(All calls charged at local rates)

How to Cope with the Stress of Student Life. **MIND (2003*).***
London: MIND.
A document with information on the different types of stress you
may encounter as a student and how to cope with them.
Weblink: http://www.mind.org.uk/Information/Booklets/How+to/
How+to+cope+with+the+stress+of+student+life.htm

7

Accommodation

What this chapter covers
Accommodation is a very important issue that needs to be tackled as soon as possible, otherwise it can become a very stressful and time-consuming problem to sort out. This chapter identifies the different types of accommodation available to you and lists the advantages and disadvantages of them all. This chapter also highlights potential disagreements which may arise in you new 'home', and how to deal with them effectively.

Finding the right place to stay

A recent survey indicates that the majority of a student's money is spent on accommodation. A student who is *not* living at home pays on average £72 a week on accommodation, which is four times what you are likely to spend on going out and entertainment. With so much money being spent on the place where you are going to live, it makes sense that you find somewhere that you like!

The main types of accommodation available to you, along with the advantages and disadvantages of each of them, are listed below.

Halls of residence/private halls

✓ Full of students/student activities going on, which can also minimise the dangers of feeling isolated and alone	✗ Can be quite noisy
	✗ No choice about whom you live with
✓ Protected environment, usually with security at the entrance	✗ Rooms can be quite small and basic
✓ Close to campus/university sites	✗ Catered halls may provide food that you don't like and be open at times which you can't make

✓ Normally has additional facilities, such as common rooms/ cleaners/ en-suite bathrooms (the facilities vary drastically from university to university, and from block to block)

✗ There are hall regulations and you will have to abide by the rules. These include how many guests you are allowed in your room, restrictions on what you can do to your room and so on

Private accommodation

✓ Your own place. You have more privacy and control over your immediate environment

✗ You need to organise yourself very quickly at the beginning of term (get the students together, find suitable accommodation etc.)

✓ Anyone can come and go, at whatever hour you please

✗ Bills need to be paid in addition to rent, so this has to be arranged among tenants

✓ Can be a great a laugh if you are with people whose company you enjoy

✗ Problems can arise if a person drops out or if you don't get along with your housemates

✓ Cook the food you want, rather than having it catered

✗ You are responsible for your own cleaning

✗ Majority of private accommodation requires payment over the holiday periods

✗ It can get very quiet

Having your own property

✓ This is usually purchased by parents for you, so you are likely to be in more control than rented accommodation

✗ Looking after your parents' property or your own is a big responsibility

✓ Instead of your money going on rent, it is paying off your family's or your own mortgage

✗ Any problems need to be sorted out by your parents or you, which can be time-consuming

✓ If it is a well-thought out investment, it can give good rental returns in the future

✗ Need to budget carefully to ensure you can pay the mortgage and bills

✗ If you are renting out to friends, it can be tricky being both a landlord and a friend

Whatever accommodation you eventually go for, avoid the last-minute panic by seeking accommodation as soon as you have been accepted by the university.

Your accommodation can have a major impact on both your work and social life, so getting the place that suits you will make a big difference on how you settle down at university. A number of first-year students do opt for student halls of residence, as it is usually a safe environment, from where you can then decide to move out if you would rather go to private accommodation. It's much harder doing it the other way round.

Dealing with conflict in your 'new' home

Whatever type of accommodation you choose, you are likely to have a conflict of interest with your neighbours or flatmates at some stage. Whether it is noisy neighbours in halls of residents or getting into the bathroom late because your flatmate takes too long, there will be times when arguments and stressful confrontations arise!

To avoid misunderstanding, it is a good idea to deal with potential problems early on. However, many students ignore the issues or behaviours because they do not want to alienate themselves from the other students by coming across as being too highly strung.

'They guys would tell me to chill out or relax, or would make an annoying comment about how it was like having their mother in the house with them! I'd laugh it off and just tidy up after them to avoid the hassle. Then one day, it just got to me. I burst out crying when I found a box of mouldy pizza under the sofa! I know I over-reacted but I couldn't help myself. Unexpectedly, it also did the trick — they hadn't realised how much the dirt round the place bugged me and were pretty apologetic too.'

Eliza, 20 years, Guildford

Situations like Eliza's can easily occur if problems are not dealt with early on. until Eliza stated that the dirt was a problem that needed to be dealt with, the other flatmates could not be blamed for not taking her seriously. In addition, by bottling up your anger or annoyance, it is more likely that your frustration will come out at an inappropriate time and over an issue that probably does not warrant your strong reaction. For example, crying does not usually assist in resolving a situation – so Eliza's outcome was rather exceptional!

Whether the issue is noise, dirt or the stealing of food from the communal fridge, being assertive can help you resolve the situation without spoiling your friendships with your neighbours or flatmates. The example below may help to illustrate one way of getting your message across assertively.

The broken record technique

This technique requires you to keep on repeating your viewpoint clearly and concisely until your message is no longer ignored. This is a particularly useful technique when someone is trying to avoid the conversation.

You: *Hi there, could you lower your music today, I can't concentrate on my work.*
Neighbour: *Hi come on in! I haven't seen you in ages!*
You: *Yeah, it's been awhile. I'd love to come in but I need to study, so if you could just turn your music down that would be great.*
Neighbour: *So you don't like my taste in music eh?*
You: *Nothing to do with what's playing, just the volume that it's at. Could you put the volume down?*
Neighbour: *Ok. No worries.*
You: *Cheers, catch up with you later!*

For more information on assertion techniques, look at Chapter 5, section 1.

Chapter summary

This chapter looked at the different types of accommodation available to you and the need to take decisive action to ensure that you have a roof over your head when you start university. It also looked at potential areas of conflict with your new neighbours or flatmates. The main areas the chapter concentrated on were:

✓ Halls of residents

✓ Private accommodation

✓ Having your own property

✓ Dealing with conflict in your new 'home': this looked at how to deal with problems with your new neighbours by using assertion techniques.

Learning points from the chapter

If you have any issues or points that you would like to remember about this chapter, please use the space provided below to note them down.

Helpful resources

StudentUK
Website: http://www.studentuk.com/Advice/accommodation.asp
Advice for student on finding and maintaining accommodation

The Student Village
Website: www.thestudentvillage.com
The student village aims to provide you with the highest standard
and friendliest student halls available.

8

Staying healthy

What this chapter covers

This chapter concentrates on your health and well-being whilst at university. Although nutritional food and exercise may not necessarily be on the top of your list of priorities, the chapter highlights the importance of staying healthy to combat stress and maintain a positive outlook. A health questionnaire is also included for you to assess how healthy your current lifestyle is.

Food for thought

Life as a student is busy and nutritional food does not tend to be high on the list of priorities. However, the take-away curries, the coffee, the biscuits and chocolate, along with the large amount of alcohol that is often associated with the student lifestyle, plays havoc with the body. Fatty foods with little nutritional value cause various heart conditions and physical impairments in older age although this is less of a problem with younger people. However, reports of early onset diabetes among the young are increasing so good nutrition is important for everybody. Individuals who are overweight are more likely to suffer from stress and depression and have lower self-esteem due to their weight.

Here are a few tips which may help you to balance your diet:

1. Eat at regular intervals – this prevents snacking.
2. Ensure your diet contains a proportion of starchy food such as bread, pasta and rice. It's cheap and has good nutritional value.
3. Eat protein such as fish when you need to get your brain in gear (i.e. when revising or taking exams). Keep the pasta for when you want to relax!
4. Eat five pieces of fruit or vegetables a day. Stick to fresh food. Not only is it cheaper than processed food, it does not contain as many additives.
5. Cut down on the fat in you diet – eat lean meat, grill rather than fry food. Low-fat cheese is preferable.
6. Reduce your sugar intake – control the amount of chocolate and sweets you eat.
7. Drink plenty of water – the recommended amount is two litres a day. Water is excellent at keeping you hydrated and healthy, which in turn makes you feel more alert. Another useful tip is to drink water whenever you feel peckish – many of us mistake the thirst signal for hunger.

By making a few small changes to your diet, within a month you will notice a change in the way you feel. What have you got to lose? Give it a go!

Eating food on the cheap

Money on food or money on entertainment? It is not always easy to make the right decision – from books, to pubs and to the clothes you wear, university can be expensive. However, there are a few practical things you can do to ensure you eat well, without having to burn a hole in your pocket!

To reduce the stress that lack of money can bring, plan a budget. Work out how much you spend on food each week and then factor that into your finances. Attempt to have a balance of fruit and vegetables as well as more traditional student foods, such as pasta and tins!

Take the time to compare prices. Supermarkets' own brands are always cheaper and keep an eye on the offer for the week. Last-minute bargains at supermarkets can be found if you go to the supermarket last thing on a Saturday when the stock is being cleared – you can often pick up quite a bargain if you are lucky!

Learn how to cook a few basic meals. Many people find that cooking is relaxing and can help you unwind after a busy day. Cooking also helps with saving money – as you know, processed meals are not only unhealthy, they are also quite expensive. Once you start cooking you will be surprised at how much cheaper it is the DIY way!

'Once I moved to self-catered accommodation I cooked a lot more! Not just for me, but for my friends too! I had two other friends who lived on campus with me, but in different accommodation. Once a week, one of us would cook, and the other two would bring a bottle. We were so tight with our money we used to have competitions on who could make the cheapest meal and who had got the best bargain on their bottle of wine! I'm sure I wouldn't touch the stuff now, but it tasted great at the time!'

Justine, 24 years, Reading

Exercise and sports

Exercise is a great reliever of stress. Over time, exercise improves both your physical and mental health. It builds up stamina, lessens fatigue (if you don't over do it), assists in anger and weight control and can reduce feelings of depression in an individual.

Here are a few tips to consider when exercising:

1. Exercise can be enjoyable! If you do not like going to the gym or aerobic classes, add an element of fun to your exercise. Your student union may run a number of classes that you can attend, from self-defence to belly dancing! So you can choose an exercise, which is a lot more interactive, entertaining, and sociable!
2. Be flexible with your exercise regime. Aim to have some exercises or sports which are not dependent on good weather conditions – the British weather is too unpredictable!
3. Integrate exercise into your daily routine. Walk instead of taking the bus to university, or take the stairs rather than using the lift.
4. Choose an activity which is fairly easy to get to from where you live. For example, traipsing across town to get to your *one hour of power* aerobics class or to reach the closest sports centre which does rock climbing, may end up being a de-motivator.
5. Don't give up! Sometimes, for reasons out of your control, you may stop your exercise routine. Stay focused and remind yourself of the reasons why you started exercising in the first place!

Exercise should be pleasurable so aim to enjoy it. Attempt not to place too many demands on yourself, such as reaching a certain target at the gym or making that ideal weight an obsession. It really isn't worth stressing yourself about it. Exercise helps you to relax and let go of all the day's tensions, so keep it simple.

How healthy are you?

To assess whether or not you lead a healthy lifestyle, fill in the following questionnaire.

How healthy are you?

Against each question below circle the answer that applies to you, where seldom is denoted by 'S', occasionally is denoted by 'O' and frequently is denoted by 'F'

Exercise scale

1.	Do you undertake physical exercise, such as jogging or cycling?	S	O	F
2.	Do you take part in sports activities that involve physical exertion?	S	O	F
3.	Do you integrate exercise into your daily routine?	S	O	F
4.	Do you feel exhausted after little physical exertion?	S	O	F

Nutrition scale

5.	Do you drink more than five cups of coffee a day?	S	O	F
6.	Do you drink more than eight cups of tea a day?	S	O	F

(Continued)

(Continued)

7.	Do you eat three meals a day?	S O F
8.	Do you eat between meals?	S O F
9.	Do you eat fruit and vegetables?	S O F
10.	Do you binge-drink alcohol?	S O F
11.	Do you eat foods high in saturated fats?	S O F

Relaxation scale

12.	Do you use relaxation techniques such as meditation?	S O F
13.	Do you use imagery exercises to help you relax?	S O F
14.	Do you feel physically tense?	S O F
15.	Do you suffer from migraines, backaches or headaches?	S O F

Miscellaneous

16.	Are you under-or overweight?	Yes No
17.	Do you drink in excess of the weekly guidelines for alcohol (14 units for women, 21 units for men*)	Yes No
18.	Do you smoke?	Yes No

Healthy answers

1 F	7 F	13 O or F
2 O or F	8 S	14 S
3 F	9 F	15 S
4 S (If O or F check with your GP)	10 S	16 No
5 S	11 S	17 No
6 S	12 O or F	18 S

If you answer any question with an undesirable response, you may want to consider changing that aspect of your behaviour or lifestyle, to become more healthier.

*These guidelines for alcohol consumption are recommended by many health professionals. The UK government recommends slightly higher amounts.
Source: Cooper and Palmer (2000)

Chapter summary

This chapter contained advice and tips on how to lead a healthy lifestyle at university. The main areas of discussion included:

✓ Food for thought: advice on how to eat a well-balanced diet with good nutritional value

✓ Eating on the cheap: how to eat good-value food and pick up last-minute bargains

✓ Exercise and sport: how to keep a healthy body to reduce your levels of stress and tension. It included tips on how to stay motivated to stick to your exercise routine

✓ How healthy are you?: a questionnaire to assess how healthy your lifestyle is

Learning points from the chapter

If you have any thoughts or comments that you would like to remember about this chapter, you can write them down in the space provided below.

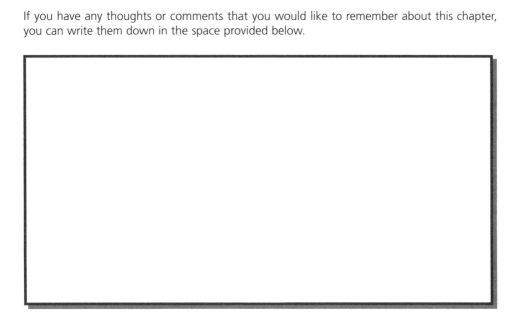

Helpful resources

British Nutrition Foundation

High Holborn House, 52–54 High Holborn, London WC1V 6RQ

Tel: 020 7404 6504

Website: www.nutrition.org.uk

Vegetarian Society

Parkdale, Denham Road, Altrincham, Cheshire WA14 4QG

Tel: 0161 925 2000 (Monday–Friday 8.30am–5pm)

Website: www.vegsoc.org

The Vegetarian Society is an educational charity promoting understanding and respect for vegetarian lifestyles.

Foodfitness

Website: www.foodfitness.org.uk

The Food and Drink Federation's website offers healthy lifestyle tips and a self-assessment questionnaire on eating and exercise habits.

Eating Disorders Association

1st Floor, Wensum House, 103 Prince of Wales Road, Norwich NR1 1DW

National helpline: 0845 634 1414 (weekdays 8.30am–8.30pm, Saturdays 1pm–4.30pm)
Helpline email: helpmail@edauk.com
Website: www.edauk.com

Eating Disorders Association is a UK-wide charity providing information, help and support for people affected by eating disorders and, in particular, anorexia and bulimia nervosa. Details of local contacts in your area are freely available to callers ringing the national helpline.

National Centre for Eating Disorders
54 New Road, Esher, Surrey KT10 9NU
Tel: 01372 469493

9

Are you on the right course?

What this chapter covers

This chapter gives advice on what to do if you realise that you are on the wrong course. Some students find that the course they have chosen does not meet their expectations and this can be a very stressful experience. This chapter offers practical advice and illustrates techniques to help you make the right decision.

Was it the right decision?

So you are beginning to settle down in your accommodation and have had a great few weeks getting introduced to student life. Now it's time to concentrate on the reason you are here – your degree course. But what happens if you find that it is not quite what you were expecting? Statistics show that about one in six students either drop out of university or seriously consider doing so. The primary reason for this was disappointment with their course and that it *'wasn't what they expected it to be'* (42 per cent). After all the hard work of getting to university, coming to the conclusion that it may be the wrong course for you can be very stressful.

However, if you genuinely feel that your course or your university isn't right for you, you will need to think carefully and act quickly to rectify the situation. Otherwise you may have to wait for the next academic year before you can make any changes.

'I started my course on Business IT and hated it! I couldn't believe how boring it was. Whilst everyone else was settling into their courses and getting to know their way around, I was running around to see what else I could do. The worst part was that I didn't know what I wanted – it was an important decision to make and I didn't have much time. What made it even more stressful was that when I tried to get on to different degrees at my university and at others, the places were all taken! It got sorted out eventually, so it was worth it. But it was horrible at the time.'

Simran, 23 years, Kingston

Talk to parents, friends and tutors to discuss your concerns and work through the possible alternatives. Contacting a trusted teacher from your old school for a chat may also be helpful.

Do your own research as well. Find out about what other courses are available and whether you are eligible for transfer on to a different or more appropriate course. The worst possible approach you can take is to pretend that there isn't a problem (sticking your head in the sand approach) or running around in a constant state of panic (the headless chicken approach), as neither tactic is likely to assist you in making the right decision.

Questions to ask yourself

If you are in a quandary about changing your degree course, ask yourself a few questions to assist you in making your decision.

- Am I feeling homesick or do I actually dislike the course?
- Would I mind taking a year out and attempting to get a place on a more appropriate course next year?
- Do I know what I would like to do instead of this course?
- Have I spoken to the lecturers on my current course to see whether I am overreacting (being the first few weeks of term you may not be into the main part of your syllabus as yet)?
- What other courses are available?
- Do I have enough time to transfer on to another course this year?
- Is there time and spaces available to transfer elsewhere to another university or college?
- Could I have an informal chat with a student in the year above me, who is on this course, to get a better idea of what my course is really like?
- If I decide to change my course, I will need to act quickly. Do I know who are the right people to talk to?

If you feel you have made the wrong choice, it is important to stay positive and think about how you can improve the situation. By staying in a positive frame of mind, thinking constructively (see Chapter 3) and keeping your goal in sight, you are likely to be more successful in achieving your desired outcome.

It is also useful to keep an open mind, remembering all the alternatives that are open to you. A choice form may be a useful way of helping you clarify the situation, as shown in the case study below.

Case study **Was it the right decision?**

George had been at university for a month before he began to question his motives for being there. The course he was on was not what he had expected but he wasn't sure whether his perception would change with time. George was beginning to settle down at university and was unsure of what he should do. He used a Making Choices form to give him more clarity of the problems he was facing.

Making Choices form

State problem or issue: Changing my degree course	
Pros	**Cons**
I would be able transfer over to a more suitable course	I don't know whether I would enjoy it any more than the one I am on already
I may be able to take a gap year and go travelling until next year	I will lose a year and I probably won't get my act together to go travelling
I could choose a university closer to home	If I do this, I may have to stay at home
I will have the opportunity to meet new people on a different course	It will probably be harder now, as people have probably already established their circle of friends
I could choose a more flexible degree which has more variety in the modules I choose	It is unlikely I will get a place on one of these degree courses now. I will probably have to wait until next year

© Centre for Coaching, 2005

Using the form gives more clarity to the situation and makes you brainstorm all the potential scenarios so you do not rush into something you are not sure of.

Have a go! Making the right decision

Think about all the options that are currently available to you. Use the Making Choices form to gain a greater insight into the advantages and disadvantages of changing your course now.

Making Choices form

State problem or issue:	
PROS	**CONS**

Chapter summary

This section looked at what you could do if you feel that the course you are on is not right for you. It included a Making Choices form to help you work out how you are going to deal with the situation.

Learning points from the chapter

If you have any thoughts or comments about this chapter, you can write them down in the space provided below.

Helpful resources

Directgov
Website: www.direct.gov.uk
Weblink: http://www.direct.gov.uk/Topics/Learning/
HigherEducationStudents/fs/en

Information to help get you started in higher education: choosing a course, help with applications and interviews, advice about student finance and graduate careers.

10

Pubs, clubs and societies

What this chapter covers

This chapter is about socialising at university. Whether you have particular hobbies, enjoy being a member of specific societies or enjoy meeting up with other students, university gives you the opportunity to do this! Having fun and relaxing is a brilliant way of reducing stress and tension. So finding social outlets that you enjoy is an important element to surviving your university years!

Making the most of your social life

With the social nights out, sports facilities and the range of societies you can join, there are few excuses for getting bored at university!

Although your first week as a fresher may seem a bit exhausting, it is probably the best time to make friends – friendship groups form quickly and by introducing yourself to as many people as possible you will make things easier for yourself in the long run. Students tend to be at their friendliest in their first week or so, making it that much easier to approach people. Research has highlighted the importance of social support as a buffer against stress so it really is worth making an effort to make friends as soon as possible.

Going to the pub is the official favourite pastime for students. So, make sure that you make your money last as long as possible, head off to the Student Union (SU) where drinks tend to be cheaper and keep an eye out for happy hours and student nights in your local pubs.

Bars and pubs are a fantastic place to get to know your new-found friends. The atmosphere can be quite relaxed and there are usually enough people to mingle with. It can also be good to start your evenings off in pubs, especially if some people are coming out on their own.

If you are into your music, make sure you find out about your local club scene. Many clubs play different types of music on different nights, aiming to cater for all tastes. Whether you are an 80s disco diva or into trance music, there are likely to be clubs in the local vicinity where you can dance the night away. Information on gigs or special promotional nights are always available from your SU.

'Our SU has different club nights practically every night of the week. One of my favourite times is Rag Week, which is a charity week full of events, competitions and club nights. A popular one is the traffic light disco where everyone wears a different coloured badge — red, amber and green funnily enough! And that's to show whether you're up for some ... companionship, or not!'

Lucy, 18 years, London

As with any nights out, when you are out in clubs, pubs or bars be wary of strangers who are acting suspiciously and keep your drink with you at all times.

As if this wasn't enough to keep you occupied, universities also have a huge range of societies you can sign up to. These range from the weird and wonderful to the more traditional. It is worth signing up to any societies you may be interested in your first few weeks at university. Freshers week is probably the best time to do this, as that is when Society members are easiest to find. Don't worry too much if you are not 100 per cent sure that you will be a dedicated society member or if your interest dwindles after the first few weeks … you won't be the first.

Joining societies are an easy way to get to know people who share the same interests as you. It is worth noting that many hobbies or activities which are usually fairly expensive to participate in (such as horse riding or abseiling) may be discounted for students. So if there is something that you have always wanted to try … now is definitely the right time!

Joining club and societies also takes away the awkwardness of having to go up to complete strangers and strike up obscure conversations, as you already have the conversation topic, and you are all interested in talking about it!

'I am a really shy person and no matter how easy everyone tells me it is, I couldn't go up to complete strangers and strike up a conversation. So whilst everyone would be happily chatting in the pub, I'd look like a moody bloke sitting in the corner with my pint! I'm a fervent table tennis player and so I joined the tennis table society and I found it so much easier to make friends. The environment didn't force the friendships, they sort of developed

over time, after a few games we'd go for a drink and so on. I've made some great friends from there.'

Scott, 19 years, Southampton

If you believe that there isn't a society that meets your needs or interests you, don't despair! You can always start your own society and apply for an annual or term-by-term budget to get it off the ground. If this is something you would be interested in doing, contact your Entertainments Officer at your SU and discuss your ideas.

'It's a great way of learning to budget in a business sense, as your aim is to make a profit and at a very minimum to stay afloat! We started a music society called Getting Hectic at Warwick. I was involved in producing flyers on the pc and distributing them in and around the SU. I used to go round to all the local pubs and restaurant to reach the widest audience. It was a fantastic way of meeting new people and I think I learnt quite a bit about running a small business.'

Jennie, 27 years, Warwick

With so many activities going on, there are great opportunities to try out new things and enjoy what your university has on offer – so don't just sit there, go on and take advantage of them!

Chapter summary

This chapter concentrated on the social activities that universities have to offer you. Being relaxed and socialising with friends are important buffers against stress, so having these outlets can really assist in keeping stress at bay.

Learning points from the chapter

If you have any thoughts or comments about this chapter, you can write them down in the space provided here.

Helpful resources

National Union for Students (London)
Nelson Mandela House, 461 Holloway Road, London N7 6LJ
Tel: 020 7272 8900
Text phone: 020 7561 6577
Email: nusuk@nus.org.uk

National Union of Students Scotland
29 Forth Street, Edinburgh EH1 3LE
Tel: 0131 556 6598
Email: mail@nus-scotland.org.uk

National Union of Students–Union of Students in Ireland
29 Bedford Street, Belfast BT2 7EJ
Tel: 028 9024 4641
Text phone: 028 9032 4878
Fax: 028 9043 9659
Email: info@nistudents.org

National Union of Students Wales (Undeb Cenedlaethol Myfyrwyr Cymru)
Windsor House, Windsor Lane, Cardiff CF10 3DE
Tel: 029 2037 5980
Email: office@nus-wales.org.uk

StudentsUK
Website: www.studentuk.com

11

Managing your money

What is covered in this chapter

This chapter looks at how to manage your finances. Money mismanagement is one of the key stressors at university. This chapter highlights the different sources of income that a student may have coming into their account, such as student loans and parental contributions, and highlights a number of methods that can be used to budget your finances, such as using a budget calculator, choosing the right bank to open your account with and listing your expenses. It also offers advice on how to deal with a friend who always wants to borrow money from you without repaying the loan! Some practical tips on how to cut your costs are also available at the end of the chapter.

Keeping track of your finances

The trouble with being poor is that it takes up all your time.
(William De Kooning, b. 1904)

Being short of money at university is not that uncommon a story. In fact, it is one of the few times in your life that being broke is quite acceptable, and to a great extent it's expected!

However, having to count your pennies all the time can become frustrating and stressful. It is important to keep track of your expenses as you have to make sure that your money lasts you through each term. But before we can analyse where all your money goes, it is useful to look first at what money is coming into your account.*

---

*Please note that although this chapter has been written with the most up-do-date information on student finances, we are aware that governments may change their policies so it is advisable to stay informed via your student finance adviser or Local Education Authority.

Student loan

Currently, for students who are living in England or Wales and studying in the United Kingdom, the Government offers a loan to assist with the expenses of living at university (such as accommodation, food and course material). From 2006, there is an additional loan to cover the cost of your tuition fees, so full-time students will no longer need to pay their fees before they start their course. Instead, the student loan that covers the cost of the tuition fees will be paid directly to their university on their behalf.

The student loans that are available are much cheaper than any loan you may be given from a high street bank as the interest rate charged is linked to inflation. This means that the amount of money you end up repaying is equivalent in real terms to the amount of money you borrowed originally. How much money you get will depend on a number of factors, including where you're going to study (students living in London are likely to get more money) and where you will be living (at home or in halls/renting). 75 per cent of the maximum loan is available to all eligible students regardless of any other income they have. However, the remaining 25 per cent of the loan amount will depend on your own income and/or that of your family. This will be assessed by your Local Education Authority (LEA). The repayments on the loan do not start until you start earning an income of £15,000 or more and the monthly repayments will also depend on the amount you will earn as opposed to the amount you have borrowed.

Other financial support

Assistance is also available to certain groups of students who may require additional help. Currently, support is available for

- Students with dependent children
- Students with dependent adults (partners, parents or other members of your family)
- Disabled students
- Students with additional travel costs
- Students who have been in care

Your university or college may be able to provide additional support for students who are having financial difficulties (hardship funds). Additional money may also be available through sponsorship from organisations or via bursaries, access funds and grants. The amount of money given varies enormously but the grants and funds are usually one-off payments and do not have to be repaid.

- Access to Learning Fund – provides extra financial help for students on low incomes who are experiencing financial difficulties.
- The Parent's Learning Allowance – to help with course-related costs for students who have dependent children. Contact your LEA.
- Child Tax Credit – students with children can claim the tax credit which is paid to parents regardless of whether they are studying or working. Contact the Inland Revenue for further information.
- Childcare grant – for full-time students with dependent children in registered or approved childcare. Contact your LEA for more information.
- Adult Dependants' grant – students with partners or other adult members of your family who depend on you financially may be able to get additional financial support. Contact your LEA for more information.
- Disabled Students' Allowances (DSAs) – additional support is available and the amount you receive is not dependent on your income or your households. The assistance given does not have to be repaid. Contact your LEA for further information.

Parental contribution

The majority of students do receive some level of support from their parents, guardians, partners of other family members (85 per cent). If you are fortunate to be supported by your parents, it's worth doing your maths to calculate approximately how much money you will require from them. This will lessen the need to keep going back to them and having the stress of grovelling for more when you hit a shortfall.

Also, the more thought you have put into the amount of money you need, the easier it is to justify it to your parents. If possible, get a set amount each month, as opposed to one lump sum. This will help you to budget and prevent you from blowing your whole term's money in the first few weeks!

Jobs

There is nothing quite like the independence of having your own source of money? Getting a job gives you a regular income and can also boost your career prospects after you graduate. It can give you confidence in the workplace and keeps you in touch with the world of work. However, juggling commitments can be stressful so be careful that you do not take on too many hours as it may end up affecting your performance on your course. Universities tend to recommend that you do not work more than 15 hours a week.

Dealing with your finances

Avoidance doesn't help!

When you get your student loan in one go it can seem like a lot of money but remember it has to last you the whole term. A common cause of stress is money mismanagement, which not only causes concern now, but can create debt for your future … do remember this fact! It does not take long to shift from not having enough money to go out, to accumulating high levels of debt that you have no way of paying off.

One of the common ways of getting into a high level of debt is **avoidance**. This is when you push the problem to the back of your mind, maybe because you are having such a good time or you just don't want to deal with the consequences. You avoid thinking of the debt you are incurring and stick your head in the proverbial sand!

'Looking back I can't believe I did it. My girlfriend was in my room one night and saw this pile of unopened letters. She asked me what they were and I just shrugged my shoulders in embarrassment. We opened all my bills, one by one, and I cringed every time I saw what was owed – most of it was interest. My girlfriend couldn't believe the situation I had got myself into. I guess I knew I was in trouble, I just didn't want to know how much!'

Nick, 25 years, Oxford

It is not surprising that just under half of all students (49 per cent) believe that having little money is the worst aspect of student life (MORI, 2005). Yet, it seems to be part and parcel of the student experience, and one that is unlikely to change! In this chapter we will concentrate on ways of managing your finances, to minimise the stress that the lack of money can cause.

Staying positive – staying in control

Unlike Nick in the quote above, problems are a lot easier to solve when you believe you have some level of control over them (see Chapter 2 for more information on 'locus of control'). By believing that you can have an effect on the outcome of a situation you ensure a much more proactive approach and improve your chances of dealing with the situation more effectively. Yet many of us go for the '*I don't want to think about it*' approach. By refusing to acknowledge of the problem, you are likely to increase your levels of stress as you see yourself as *helpless* in the situation and let the problem get the better of you.

Budgeting

Surviving university without a certain level of budgeting can be financially hazardous! However, it can be quite hard to keep track of what your money is being spent on unless you start off getting into good financial habits. Once you start budgeting it soon becomes quick and easy to keep tabs on what is coming into your account and also reduces the stress of debits from your account! Below are a few techniques to help you budget more effectively.

Listing your expenses

This may seem a bit tedious to begin with, but it is great way of staying aware of how much money is being spent and on what. It also highlights areas where you can cut down on spending and sometimes (when you're lucky) show you when you may have a little bit of extra cash to play around with!

Begin by listing your income and expenditure. Compile a list with two columns. In the first column write down what money you are expecting to come in during the month, for example your student loan, money from home, pay from your part-time job and so on. In the second column, list the payments you have to make throughout the month, such as accommodation (the biggest expense for most students!), bills (e.g. electricity, gas, mobile phone and any other direct debits), food expenses, credit card payments, toiletries, clothes, money for books or stationery, money for going out, travel expenses, music and any other miscellaneous expenses. It's worth noting down all your costs, big or small, as this all helps to give a better picture of how you spend your money.

To make your expenses list even easier the Department for Education and Skills come up with an interactive web tool called a budget calculator. You can access the calculator by going to the following web address: http://www.aimhigher.ac.uk/student_finance/cost_of_living_calculator.cfm. This tool makes budgeting a lot easier as all you need to do is put in the amount of money you spend on various living costs during a term and during a week. It then calculates your weekly and per term expenditure and the balance you have, based on the figures you have put in. It is a simple and fast way of giving you an overview of your financial situation.

Being assertive with friends

'I'm broke, can I borrow some cash?'

It is all too easy to be over-supportive of our friends. Many students find themselves a bit strapped for cash and in need of some financial assistance from friends. But the problem arises when friends are perpetually broke and in consistent need of your money!

Even if you enjoy their company, having a mate who never repays money you have lent to them soon begins to wear your friendship down. You may find it useful to consider what choices you have in dealing with such a situation:

1. Continue to give them free credit and whinge about it.
2. Continue to give them free credit and don't whinge about it.
3. Avoid their company and run a mile in the opposite direction when you next see them.
4. Become resentful.
5. Become assertive and calmly state, *'I'm not prepared to give you any more money'*, when they next make a request. You may need to repeat this a few times to get the message over.

In the long term, option 5 is probably the best approach if you want to maintain your friendship and not be resentful of their behaviour. Section 1 in Chapter 5 offers advice on assertion techniques and provides a number of assertiveness methods which you can practise. In the end, if your assertive attitude is not well received, then may be it is worth asking yourself whether that person was a real friend anyway.

Smart banking

When you open an account at a high street bank, resist the goodies until you have found out what the account itself actually offers. The interest rate they charge is one of the main things to look out for:

- Which bank gives you the highest interest-free overdraft?
- Who has the best authorised overdraft interest rate?
- Compare different banks' interest rates on unauthorised borrowing.

Once you have done this, then go for the most appealing extras that they are offering! Some students also find it useful to open a second account. By doing this, you can put all your incoming money in to one account (e.g. your student loan and other incoming monies which you may receive at the beginning of term) and transfer a set amount of money each month to the other account for your day-to-day expenses, which would cover your living and social expenses. This is likely to help you budget more effectively.

Cutting your costs

This may not be fun, but by showing a bit of restraint and discipline, you will reduce your stress by making your money last longer. Here are a few tips on how to manage your money more effectively:

- Learn how to cook. There are plenty of simple cook books to help you create healthy food cheaply and quickly.
- Carry your student union card everywhere. It can get you discounts on all sorts of things (such as 10 per cent discount in some high street retailers).
- Buy a Young Persons Railcard or bus pass if you do a lot of travelling.
- Buy the supermarket's own brands.
- Limit the amount of money you have on you. Some students find it helpful to withdraw all the money they are going to spend in the week and stick to that amount. This way you can see how much you have got left and whether you can afford that extra pint or not.
- Avoid the use of credit cards or use them in emergency situations only.
- Rather than buying all the books on your reading lists, take some of them out of the library or search out second-hand books. This can save you a small fortune. A good place to find second-hand books is at your course or departmental notice boards. Some universities also have a second-hand book shop on site which will sell you books from last year's students at very reasonable prices. Alternatively, get together with other students on your course and buy one book each from the reading lists – then share the books between you.
- Limit your nights out – it's easier to resist temptation to spend that way.
- Check you are not paying tax on your savings if you are not going to be earning any money during the financial year.
- Keep store point cards and collect points to get savings on products or cash back (e.g. Club cards or Advantage cards).
- Get student discounts on prescriptions, dental care and health checks.

Chapter summary

Managing finances is a stressful business, especially as you have the time, the places and the energy to enjoy your money but just don't have the income! This chapter emphasised the need to budget and highlighted some tips on how to make your money last.

✓ Money coming in: this includes your student loan, other financial support you may be entitled to, parental contributions and income you may receive if you take on a part-time job

✓ Money going out: this looked at ways you can manage your finances and included information on budgeting, smart banking and easy tips to cut down your costs

Learning points from the chapter

Use the space provided below to note down any useful hints or advice you have found in this chapter for reducing your stress levels.

Helpful resources

Student Loans Company (SLC)
100 Bothwell Street, Glasgow G2 7JD
Tel: 0800 405010
Website: www.slc.co.uk

Department for Education and Skills
Link to details about student loans and financial support available
at: www.dfes.gov.uk/studentsupport/students/index.shtml

Consumer Credit Counselling Service
Wade House, Merrion Centre, Leeds LS2 8NG
Helpline: 0800 328 1813 (Monday–Friday 8am–8pm)
This is a dedicated helpline for students worried about debt and
money problems. Calls and advice given are free.
Website: www.cccs.co.uk

Free Stuff
Website: www.freestudentstuff.com
A website containing free information and offers such as free
cinema tickets, free ringtones, cash for completing surveys, discount
offers and much more 'free stuff'!

Part 4   Getting down to work

In Part 4 of the handbook, we concentrate on the three main assessment procedures used by universities to monitor the progress of students.

Chapter 12 looks at how the stress of assignments can be reduced by high-lighting common problems students may have and how to address them. For example, time management skills, thinking skills and imagery are all explained as methods to overcome one of your worst enemies … procrastination!

The stress of presentations is explored in Chapter 13. It highlights techniques and practical tips to give you the confidence to perform and to help you reduce your stress and anxiety levels.

Chapter 14 covers the biggest pressure university students face – examinations! The chapter discusses why exams are so stressful and how positive thinking, effective revision techniques and maintaining routines all help in getting those desired grades!

As Part 4 deals with the academic aspects of university, by the time you have finished reading this section of the handbook, we hope you will feel more confident in preparing for your studies and approaching your work with a realistic, yet positive frame of mind.

12

Dealing with assignments

What is covered in this chapter

This chapter concentrates on how to deal with assignments and focuses on the skills required to manage your time effectively (such as prioritising, using activity lists and timetables). It also highlights the problem of procrastination and how this is likely to impact on your stress levels. Motivation imagery, thinking skills and self-acceptance are also highlighted as ways to alleviate stress when doing assignments.

Tackling assignments

No matter what course you take, the stress of doing coursework and assignments is likely to be there! On many degree courses, essays and other forms of coursework are used as evidence that a student has understood a topic area and usually form part of the final mark for the module being studied.

Coursework at university can seem quite different from school and college assignments. No one is checking how you are getting on with the work and you are left to manage your studies independently, researching topics on your own and deciding what information is relevant to you. Although autonomy and independence are usually a good way of learning, it can also be quite stressful when you are not getting the same amount of guidance that you are used to.

'There is no direction from the lecturers with the coursework. You are just given a few titles, a deadline and told to get on with it. At first I thought it was crazy – how are you supposed to know which books or journal articles are going to be useful? I learnt quickly enough though and don't photocopy everything in sight anymore!'

John, 21 years, Sussex

Coursework is an integral part of studying and you need to make time to study to ensure you are successful in your long-term goals. The following section gives you a few pointers on how to help you prepare for coursework and highlights techniques to prevent you burning the candle at both ends one night before the work is due in!

Being prepared

Coursework rarely takes students by surprise. Lecturers and tutors usually give advance warning and reasonable timescales to complete assignments. But a common habit you may slip into is leaving coursework until later, as you are under the impression that you have 'loads of time'. Yet before you know it, more coursework piles up from other modules. Being a social butterfly becomes a full-time occupation and suddenly the deadlines are looming and you're not sure how to keep your head above water! The stress begins!

Many of us have experienced the above scenario at some point and we probably all know how to resolve the last-minute stress – get organised. Staying on top of our work, balancing our commitments and preventing last-minute panic are all possible with good organisational skills and a willingness to give time management a go.

Prioritising your workload

As soon as a coursework deadline is given make sure you write it down so you don't forget it. Find out whether the coursework counts towards your final mark and by how much. It is then up to you to organise your time. One of the most effective tried-and-tested methods is to timetable the work into your daily routine.

A timetable showing your daily activities or commitments, other coursework deadlines, and when you have some spare time can help you to allocate specific time periods to your current coursework. Remember to be realistic about the time slots for your work, as they need to be at times when you feel alert and are able to concentrate. For example, if you are never up before 10am, there is no point penning in a slot from 8am to 10am, even if it is with the best of intentions!

Similarly, if you have children, choose a time when they are sleeping or not likely to be with you as opposed to times when they may want your attention. If you allocate inappropriate time slots for studying, you may find yourself becoming anxious when you are unable to sit down and get on with your work. So it is important to factor this in.

Once you have prepared a timetable, put it up in a place where you can easily see it so it's not a case of *out of sight out of mind*. Then it's time to put it into action. Initially it may seem slightly artificial or a bit restrictive but after a week or so, you will probably notice that you are able to juggle all your commitments and your studies much more effectively. Do not worry if you slip up and miss a slot on your timetable, just pick up from where you left off and start again.

An activity list

If you do not have the time to do a timetable, or find that your priorities change on a daily basis so a timetable is more difficult to organise, an activity list maybe more appropriate for you. Make a list of all the chores and activities that you want to complete in the day. Then rank each one in order of importance. The most important item will be ranked with a '1' and the second most important with a '2' and so on. Then write the list out again, but this time in order of priority.

By ensuring that you are doing the most important jobs first, and ticking the jobs off the list as you complete them, you will reduce your stress and anxiety levels. Even if you are unable to complete everything on your list, you are less likely to worry too much as the items lower down on your list are not your main priorities for the day. This is illustrated in the case study below.

Case study Activity list

Jane had a busy day ahead of her. To make it easier for her to remember what was very important for her to do and what she would like to do if she had the time, she created an activity list.

Jane found the activity list particularly useful because unlike when she normally does a 'to do' list, she had listed the most important things first. This meant that she was focused on getting the most important tasks done first.

Activity list

Tasks to do	Ranking
Do a food shop	5
Do my laundry	6
Return my library books	3
Get some money out of the bank	1
Photocopy reading material for essay	4
Phone Clare	7
Complete economics assignment	2
Tasks to do in order	
Get some money out of the bank	1
Complete economics assignment	2
Return my library books	3
Photocopy reading material for essay	4
Do a food shop	5
Do my laundry	6
Phone Clare	7

Have a go! Activity list

An activity list can be a very useful way of prioritising your day or week! List all the priorities that you have for the day. Rank each of the items on the list in order of importance. Then write the list down again, this time in the correct order in which items should be undertaken.

Activity list

Tasks to do	Ranking

Tasks to do in order

Know your topic area

Attending the lecture or having lecture notes on the topic area of your coursework may give you a good starting point, but you will need to do much more research to get a good grade. Go through the reading lists provided by the lecturer and pick out the ones you feel would be most appropriate. It is worth going to the library as soon as you have the reading list, as it is not long before all the good books get taken out. As well as books, journals, the internet and CD-Roms are all useful references, so there is no need to stick to just the reading list. Be proactive when researching your material.

To do a good piece of work it is imperative that you understand what you are writing about. This may sound obvious, but without a good grasp of the subject matter it is hard to form opinions on, or enjoy learning about, your topic. Although you are working towards a good grade, if you take an active interest in what you are learning about, you are much more likely to be motivated to produce a good piece of work.

Another useful way of obtaining information for your coursework is by talking to other students. Sharing thoughts and ideas gives you a greater grasp of the topic and may also highlight different perspectives of approaching the work.

However, if you find you are struggling with the coursework, do not be afraid to say so. Remember, that if you are having difficulties it is likely that there are other students in the same position too. Talk to other students and your tutor if you are concerned. Tutors and lecturers are there to help you and usually have allocated time periods for you to contact them if you have any queries or would like to talk to them.

Getting started

When you know you have a coursework deadline looming, what is it that makes it so difficult to sit down and do it?

Avoidance or procrastination

However much you may enjoy your subject, an essay or research project still constitutes work and we can all find things that we would rather be doing! Going to the pub, meeting friends and even doing household chores all seem more attractive or important than studies when faced with putting pen to paper.

Although procrastination is a common behaviour and you have probably found yourself doing this at some time or another, it hinders your performance on a task. So why do you do it?

FIGURE 12.1
Procrastination chart (Cooper and Palmer, 2000)

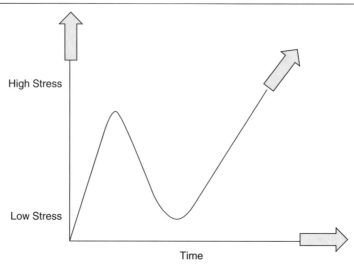

Whenever you have a task in which you want to perform well, your personal stress levels increase when you think of it. You try and avoid it for as long as possible, because thinking about it makes you feel uncomfortable or uneasy. When you change tack, for example by cleaning your room, or going for a food shop, your stress levels temporarily drop, making you feel more relaxed and calm. But, once you stop procrastinating and start thinking about doing the task, your stress levels rise higher than they did before. By delaying doing the inevitable, you put your body under further unnecessary pressure.

As illustrated in Figure 12.1, when you start to think about a challenging task, your stress levels rise. However, if you start procrastinating, your stress levels drop and you begin to feel better. This is effective at bringing down your stress and anxiety … but not for long! As soon as you let yourself think of the task, not only do your stress levels go up again, but they rise higher than they were before you started diverting your attention! This is because you realise you have less time to make the deadline. Procrastination ends up causing you a greater amount of stress and tension than if you just got on with the task in the first place.

However, even when you overcome the procrastination and sit down to do your work, are you concentrating on the assignment or do you sometimes find yourself daydreaming?

'With coursework, I do try and get down to it – I make an effort. But there are times I just end up wasting my time – looking out of the window or having a smoke and before

I know it – it's time to eat or something. One of the most irritating things that happens sometimes is when I'm reading. I'll be sitting in front of the books and would've read like page after page and then about half an hour later I realise – wait a sec, I have no idea what I've just been reading! And then I have to go back and do it all again.'

Mark, 18 years, Brighton

So, even if you have the best intentions in the world, it is likely that sometimes you may find yourself in a similar position to Mark, where you are unable to concentrate on the work – you just don't feel motivated. Although this is perfectly natural and we all find ourselves in this situation once in a while, it is not particularly helpful if you have deadlines looming and the assignments need to be done.

It is interesting to note that Mark mentions that he *tries* to study. As mentioned in Chapter 1, trying may denote effort, but it rarely marks success! Mark is more likely to be fruitful with his studies if he maintains a *'can do'* as opposed to a *'try to'* attitude towards his work.

One technique which can help you to get in the mood is motivation imagery.

Motivation imagery

This technique is used to motivate people into action (Palmer and Neenan, 1998) and can be applied to any given situation or problem. The technique highlights the impact of doing nothing compared to seeing your goals through.

Method

Think about the coursework that you have to hand in.

Now imagine that you do not do it. What impact is this likely to have on you? Will you regret it if you do not complete the coursework? How is this likely to make you feel? What will your fellow students think? How do you think your lecturer will react?

Now imagine doing the course work. How would completing the coursework affect the module? Could it give you more confidence for the next piece of work you do? Is it worth completing? How does it impact on your aspirations at university?

Finally consider how you are going to do your coursework now. For example, timetable it into your daily routine, research the topic area, talk to the lecturer to get some more information.

Please note that the order of the exercise must stay the same, beginning with imagining that you do *not* complete the work, followed by imagining the coursework has been done. Only then can it aid your motivation to carry out the task.

Case study **Motivation imagery**

Mark is a first-year undergraduate student. He has taken a module in a subject that he isn't particularly enjoying but it is important for him to pass the module as it will impact on his final year marks. He uses motivation imagery to help him get started!

What's the task?

The coursework is due in one week's time. It is a 1500-word assignment and the tutor has given three assignment options.

What if I don't do it?

Mark thinks about not doing the coursework. If he doesn't do the work he will have to come up with a good excuse to the lecturer, which is a bit of a hassle. He doesn't mind doing that, but he knows that all he can ask for is an extension – not an exemption from doing it! He thinks about other people in his lecture. A lot of them weren't ecstatic about doing the essay, but, they were getting on with it. If he got away with not writing the essay (which he rationally knew he wouldn't!), it wouldn't be very fair on the others. Mark starts to imagine in his mind's eye what might happen in the future. If he doesn't do the coursework and refuses to do it at a later date, he may even be taken off the course. This will obviously affect his first-year grades and may eventually impact upon his chosen career.

What if I do it?

Mark pictures himself actually doing the essay. It is only 1500 words and will take three afternoons to complete. He has already chosen the essay title he wants to do and has even photocopied the reading material, so all the arduous stuff has already been done. It is a fairly easy essay to write and if he does well in it, it will bump up his final-year mark, as he did poorly in the last essay he wrote. As this is the last essay in the module, it will be out of the way and he won't have to deal with this topic again! He can see how this simple step can have a positive impact upon his degree results which could positively influence his future career. Mark decides it will be a lot simpler to just sit down and get on with it.

How am I going to do it?

Mark decides on how he is going to start the coursework. He has already allocated three afternoons for it, so it isn't eating into his own time. He decides that he will contact a few friends to make sure he is on the right lines with his ideas about the essay. In addition, he will search the internet for other information which is not on the reading list. He will also create a skeleton structure for his essay and then just get on with it! Once he has completed the task he will reward himself by going to the pub with a couple of mates.

Have a go! Motivation

Think about a task or piece of coursework that you have been putting off or avoiding for some time. Use the *Get Motivated* table below to think of the benefits of not doing it and avoiding it indefinitely. Then think about the benefits of doing it sooner rather than later. If you decide it makes more sense to get on with the assignment, then put together an action plan of how and when you are going to begin it.

(Continued)

(Continued)

WHAT'S THE TASK?

WHAT IF I *DON'T* DO IT?

WHAT IF I DO IT?

HOW AM I GOING TO DO IT?

Although we do not have an option on the coursework we are given, or the timescales in which it is to be completed, we do have control over how we *think* of the assignment and how we *choose* to approach it.

Remember your thinking skills

Your thoughts are very powerful, so you need to be aware of what you say to yourself and how this may affect your emotions. Where negative thoughts exist your stress levels are likely to be higher, so learning to rephrase statements in a more helpful way will help you to regain control and assist you in dealing with your coursework more effectively. Constructive thinking will also help you in most other aspects of your life. For example:

'*There is so much information – I don't know where to start*' may well be a true reflection of how you are feeling, yet it also engenders thoughts of helplessness and panic which are not conducive to getting the work done. It would be much more useful to think in a more positive way: '*If I divide the coursework into manageable chunks, I'll have less information to deal with all at once.*'

Keep a check on your negative thinking and do not be so harsh on yourself. May be you can ask yourself the following questions:

- What advice would you give to a friend if they were feeling overwhelmed with coursework?
- Is the problem really that bad, or are you exaggerating its importance?

One particular type of negative thinking which often causes stress and pressure when completing coursework is perfectionism. This is discussed in more detail below.

Perfectionism

Perfectionism is a dangerous state of mind in an imperfect world. (Robert Hillyer)

- Do you ever feel that what you accomplish is never quite good enough?
- Do you ever find yourself working on an assignment for weeks and then having to rush through the majority of it in a last-minute panic just to get it in on time?
- Do you feel you must give more than 100 per cent on everything you do because otherwise you will be mediocre or even a failure?

If you find yourself nodding your head to any of the above questions, you may find that you are not simply being conscientious and ambitious but you may in fact be striving for perfection. Although being a high achiever can be desirable, a perfectionist type of attitude can rob you of your sense of personal satisfaction and cause you to fail to achieve.

When you find yourself putting perfectionist demands on yourself, ask yourself the following types of questions:

- Am I being realistic? Or am I placing too many demands on myself?
- Should I be focusing on the outcome I want rather than what other people expect of me?
- Does everyone agree with me? Are they thinking in the same way? If not, why don't they?

It is important to recognise your accomplishments and learn from any past mistakes. This should replace any negative thinking. Accept that you do have limitations and, if necessary, ask for help.

What if you do not complete an assignment?

Life is not always predictable and there may be occasions when you do not complete an assignment on the date it is due. If you are aware of potential problems with the deadline date, or find that you are struggling to complete the assignment, it is advisable to talk to the lecturer who gave the assignment as soon as you can. They may extend the deadline date or give you further assistance if you are having difficulties. However, if you do not approach them and miss the deadline date, they are less likely to be sympathetic to your cause.

Unless your circumstances are out of the ordinary, it may be worth exploring why you were unable to complete the assignment within the given timeframe. If your reasons appear to be linked to your feelings of self-worth, such as believing that your lecturer thinks you are incompetent, then it is useful to think about how you view yourself.

Self-acceptance

If you were to think about the things which make you a *good* person to be around, what types of reason would you give? Would it be because:

- you make people laugh?
- you have money?
- you are a high achiever?
- you're loved by others?
- you have achieved a lot in your life?
- you are attractive?
- you are a good parent or friend?

All of the reasons outlined above are factors which are external to yourself. So feeling good about yourself can be based on something which can change over time. For example, you may break up with your partner or fail an exam and all of a sudden you are questioning two of the reasons why you think you are a *good* person (i.e. you are loved by others and you are a high achiever).

By creating your identity on factors which can change over time, you will inevitably become disillusioned with yourself when potential problems arise which confront your self-esteem. This is often seen when rich people become bankrupt. They lose their status and they often become vulnerable because they lose their sense of worth at the same time.

So, how can you feel good about yourself without basing your judgements on external attributes? By self-acceptance. Self-acceptance acknowledges that one of the key aspects that makes you human is that you are fallible and not perfect. It is based on an inner judgement of yourself as opposed to any achievements or accomplishments you have gained during your lifetime.

So, for example, if you did not hand in your assignment because you thought *'If my lecturer gives me a bad grade on my assignment, I am incompetent'*, you would be basing your opinion of yourself on an external factor. However, if you are self-accepting, you may have this thought: *'If my lecturer gives me a bad grade on my assignment, it will highlight areas or skills that I need to work on but it will not mean that I'm a totally incompetent person'*. Here, you are rating your ability or behaviour and not you as an individual. By using this method you accept that you are fallible and identify your problem without de-motivating yourself.

Working on an assignment: quick tips

Whether you are writing an essay, review or evaluating a piece of work, remember that the aim of the coursework is to highlight your knowledge and understanding. Below are a few tips on what to remember when approaching your coursework.

✓ Start your coursework whilst the ideas are still fresh in your mind.

✓ Choose a sensible place and time to start working, where you are unlikely to be distracted.

✓ Make sure you understand the question being asked in your assignment.

✓ Use clear and easy-to-understand language.

✓ Do not waffle just to get the word count up – you are unlikely to get additional marks for it, and the point you are making might get lost in the words!

✓ Stick to a clear structure. Have a clear beginning, middle and end. If the course has a specific structure you need to adhere to – use it.

✓ Write a skeleton draft of the essay or discussion. This helps you keep to a structure that is methodical and well-thought out. It also ensures that you stay focused on the question.

Chapter summary

Dealing with assignments can be stressful, especially when you have more than one to do and they all seem to have the same deadline date! This chapter offered advice on managing your workload:

✓ Being prepared: this included completing activity lists and knowing your topic area

✓ Dealing with procrastination: this section described why procrastination increased your stress levels and explored techniques to help you get in the mood to study. Techniques included motivation imagery, thinking skills and self-acceptance

The chapter also included quick tips and advice to help you work more effectively on an assignment.

Learning points from the chapter

Use the space provided below to note down any useful advice or techniques you have found in this chapter that can help reduce your stress levels.

Helpful resources

The Study Skills Handbook. Cottrell, S. (2003).
Basingstoke: Palgrave Macmillan.
A book which provides useful advice and practical exercises to help students develop their study skills.

The Speed Reading Book. Buzan, T. (2000). London: BBC Worldwide
Buzan discusses his various approaches to reading, study, concentration and learning. Numerous self-tests and practical examples enable readers to assess their progress at each stage. With its flexible approach this book shows that reading speeds of over 1000 words per minute are possible.

The Student Skills Guide. Drew, S. and Bingham, R. (2004).
Aldershot: Gower.
This guide outlines key skills for students, including reflecting on your experience, critical analysis, learning styles and successful participation in seminars and meetings.

13

Handling presentations

What this chapter covers
This chapter focuses on presentation skills. Giving presentations can trigger so much angst for students. There are tips on how to prepare for your presentation and ways of dealing with the stress and anxiety that presentations evoke. The use of a daily thought record, imagery and relaxation are mentioned to assist in dealing with the stress of doing presentations.

The fear of presentations

'Being a fairly large lady I have always been far too self-conscious for presentations! I actually chose a course where I thought I wouldn't have to do anything like that – can you believe it? When I stand in front of people I feel like they are all staring at my bust or something rather than listening to what I am saying! I just hate having all those eyes on me. Of course I have had to do presentations and my first one was really tough. But I had friends around me who helped me to handle my paranoia! I wore black baggy clothes and looked at the back of the room when addressing the group which made me less 'on display'! I'm still no fan of presentations, but by keeping it all in perspective and obviously with tonnes of practice I get through them!'

Roz, 25 years, Newcastle

If the prospect of doing a presentation makes you feel a bit nervous, don't despair – you are not alone! Standing in front of an audience, being an 'expert' on the information being presented, can be a daunting experience. Yet, many of you will need to do presentations as part of your degree courses and being skilful at doing presentations is likely to be very handy once you join the world of work.

If you get very anxious or apprehensive about doing a presentation, it is likely that the stress response will come into play (see Chapter 1 for more details). The mere thought of doing a presentation may begin to make you feel depressed and stressed out. You may begin to suffer from physical signs of stress (such as racing heart, ulcers, restlessness) and it may even affect your sleeping patterns (look at the effects a forthcoming presentation had on Amy in Chapter 1). Yet doing a presentation does not need to be that nerve-racking, and many individuals manage to overcome their fear of presentations with a few simple techniques such as positive thinking, coping imagery, relaxation and, let's not forget, practice!

The different stages of a presentation

If you are worried about doing a presentation, spend some time thinking about all the different aspects of doing it that make you anxious. You may find it easier to break down the different stages of doing a presentation and see how you respond to thinking about the different bits of it. For example:

Preparation of the presentation – Are you worried about the content of the presentation? Will it contain the right facts, be the right length and be interesting? What stress-provoking thoughts are going through your head at the moment?

Talking – How do you feel about doing the presentation, standing in front of fellow students and/or strangers. Do you feel uncomfortable about this? What are the thoughts and images going through your mind? How do you feel about talking in front of an audience? Do you feel self-conscious?

Making a mistake – Are you concerned about losing your place, your mind going blank or other such mistakes during the presentation? What would be the worst part of making such a mistake? How would you feel about it?

Answering questions – Are you apprehensive about the questions you may be asked after the presentation? Are you concerned that you may not be able to answer a question or look incompetent if you do not give a sufficient answer? What concerns do you have about answering questions after a presentation?

The idea of the exercise is to identify the thoughts that are making you feel anxious about doing the presentation. Once you have identified them, you will need to spend some more time challenging these thoughts and thinking of more appropriate and helpful beliefs which will keep your stress levels lower.

To help you think of the stress-inducing thoughts (SITs) you can use the daily thought record. This is an effective way of eliciting instant feelings for a situation because it requires you to write down your immediate thoughts without thinking about it too much.

Daily thought record

The daily thought record is used in cognitive coaching or therapy to help people monitor and challenge unhelpful thinking. For this exercise imagine yourself doing a presentation and think of any thoughts that come into your head immediately.

These immediate thoughts are sometimes called automatic thoughts and when you are stressed they are usually unhelpful and negative. You then need to rate them (from 0–100 per cent) in terms of how strongly you believe in the thought.

Once you have noted down and rated your unhelpful thoughts, you need to think of ways to develop more helpful and constructive thoughts. Use your thinking skills and imagery to help you come up with a more effective way of thinking. This is similar to the six-step approach discussed in Chapter 3 (see page 34). Some people prefer this variation of the method.

The case study below illustrates the method of eliciting your unhelpful thoughts and developing more helpful and constructive thoughts.

Case Study Daily thought record: Jane's thought record on doing a presentation

Situation	Unhelpful thoughts	Emotions	Helpful response
1. Describe actual event leading up to unpleasant emotion or 2. Stream of thoughts, daydreams or memories 3. Distressing physical sensations	1. Write down any thought(s) that came into your head before the emotion(s) 2. Rate your belief in automatic thought(s) 0–100%	1 Specify the emotion you feel – are you anxious, angry, sad and so on? 2. Rate the degree of the emotion you feel 0–100	1. Write down a helpful response to counter the unhelpful thought(s) 2. Rate your belief in the new helpful response 0–100% 3. Re-rate emotions 0–100
Event: Speaking in front of a group of people	*Thought:* I'm giving it away by blushing – everyone can see how vulnerable I am (80% belief in thought)	Anxious – 80 (hot flushes, stomach churning, trembling)	No one will think I'm stupid if I blush. This is not abnormal. Although it would be desirable if I didn't – 75% belief in thought
	Thought: It's my turn next. Oh God, oh no … Bloody hell! (65% belief in thought)	Panicky – 80	Block other negative thoughts with 'IT'S NO BIG DEAL' – 80% belief in thought
	Thought: My mind is going blank. I can't stand being embarrassed (90% belief in thought)	Embarrassment – 60 (stomach churning)	I can stand it. Deep breaths to be taken when my stomach is churning or if I feel sick or dizzy – 65% belief in thought

(Continued)

(Continued)

Situation	Unhelpful thoughts	Emotions	Helpful response
	Thought: I've got to do this right (75% belief in thought)	Anxious – 80	I've only done this a few times before so it is reasonable to make a mistake – 75% belief in the thought I now only feel only 30 embarrassed; 40 anxious

Have a go!

Imagine yourself doing a presentation that you are anxious about. By doing this, you are more likely to provoke the same sensations you would feel if you were actually standing in front of your audience (although the feelings will probably be less intense). Rate these thoughts between 1 and 100 per cent. Identify any emotions you feel in relation to the thoughts (e.g. anger, anxiety or fear) and rate how strongly you feel the emotion between 0 and 100. Then think of a more helpful thought to replace your negative thought. This needs to be something you believe is true. Rate this new thought between 0 and 100 per cent.

Have a go! Daily thought record

Use the daily thoughts record to write down your negative automatic thoughts (NATs) as well as your new rational and helpful beliefs. This will help you to deal with your anxieties more effectively.

(Continued)

(Continued)

Daily Thought Record

Situation	Unhelpful thoughts	Emotions	Helpful response
1. Describe actual event leading up to unpleasant emotion or 2. Stream of thoughts, daydreams or memories 3. Distressing physical sensations	1. Write down any thought(s) that came into your head before the emotion(s) 2. Rate your belief in automatic thought(s) 0–100%	1 Specify the emotion you feel – are you anxious, angry, sad and so on? 2. Rate the degree of the emotion you feel 0–100	1. Write down a helpful response to counter the unhelpful thought(s) 2. Rate your belief in the new helpful response 0–100% 3. Re-rate emotions 0–100

Coping imagery

Many of us think in *pictures* or *images*. We visualise an event or situation which has occurred or is yet to occur in the future (see Chapter 4 for more information).

To use the coping imagery technique you need to imagine yourself in the feared situation, but dealing with the concerns you have. So, for example, imagine yourself walking in front of the class and then dropping all your notes. But also imagine yourself making a quick comment and picking up each paper and putting them back in order. By imagining the worst possible scenarios, you confront your fears because you are addressing your most dreaded eventuality in your mind.

Step 1 – Think of a future presentation, discussion, meeting or event you are worried about – for example, doing a book review in front of your tutor group.

Step 2 – Note down aspects of the presentation that you are most stressed about – for example, my mind's going to go blank; I will feel sick; I won't be able to answer the questions at the end and I'll look like I don't really understand what I've been talking about!

Step 3 – Develop ways of dealing with it – for example, if my mind goes blank, pause for a minute (maybe even have a sip of water to gain a few seconds). If I still don't remember, I can have a look through the cue cards to find my place again.

If I feel sick, remember to use the breathing techniques learned in Chapter 4. Remind myself that it isn't a big deal if I don't do the presentation perfectly and bring myself back to a level of calm.

If I can't answer a question, imagine telling the person that they have asked a good question and that I don't have the information on me, but will get back to them with the answer later. Remember my thinking skills, and ask myself whether people will really think I'm a bit stupid for not knowing the answer? What would I think if someone said that to me if I asked a question?

If you find that you are having difficulties to think of new ways of dealing with the stressful aspects of the presentation, ask friends and colleagues how they would handle that situation. This brainstorming is likely to give you a different approach to tackle the problem and may even highlight how common your fears are!

Whatever way you approach the task, remember to be honest to yourself. Think of the worst possible outcome that you are worried about. By eliciting your most feared eventualities you will be in a better position to tackle all your worries and prevent negative images becoming self-fulfilling prophecies.

Step 4 – Now practise visualising these new ways of dealing with the situation in your mind's eye.

Step 5 – Practise your coping imagery regularly, especially when you are feeling stressed about the presentation.

Relaxation

Relaxation is always advisable when you are feeling under pressure and strain. It is particularly useful when used in conjunction with other techniques. For example, before you begin practising your coping imagery it may be useful to do a relaxation exercise (see Chapter 4 for more detail). So when you conjure up your negative images of the presentation in your mind, you are already in a more relaxed state to deal with the problem more effectively. As with any technique, it requires time and practice. You may not get the desired effects straight away – stick with it and over time you will be able to see the positive impact it has on you.

Practical tips for doing a presentation

Preparing for the presentation

- Be clear on the objectives of your presentation – what is your audience's knowledge base? How much background information will they need? What are the key points that need to be made?
- Use cue cards with key points or phrases to make sure the main points are addressed.
- Make the story flow – if you jump from one idea to another, you will lose the audience in the confusion.
- Practise your presentation out loud – you may find it useful initially to practise in front of a mirror by yourself or to get your housemates or friends to sit down and listen to it.

Visual aids

- Make slides simple – they are there to help you explain a point
- Pictures tend to be more memorable
- Have no more than five bullet points per visual
- Use key words as opposed to sentences
- Have the font size quite large (18pts)
- Use colour, but avoid orange and yellow as they don't show up very well. It may also be worth bearing in mind that people with colour blindness may confuse reds and greens too.

Making the presentation

- You have probably heard this before, but it is very useful to keep it in mind – '*Tell the audience what you are going to tell them, then tell them, then remind them what you have just told them*'
- Keep the presentation short
- Keep the language simple and easy to understand
- Leave time at the end of the presentation for questions – if you don't understand a question, ask the person to rephrase it!

The delivery

- Speak clearly – not too soft or loud. Judge the acoustics in the room you are presenting in. If in doubt, ask the audience
- Look at your audience. If this makes you feel uncomfortable, scan the room for familiar faces who can give you reassuring smiles. If this is not possible, just look above everyone's head – this gives the impression you are having eye contact with the audience
- Avoid jokes unless you are a natural. It is particularly important to avoid amusing stories or jokes if the jokes do not relate to the topics you are discussing or if you are very nervous about doing the presentation
- Pause at key points – this not only emphasises the point being made but wakes people up
- Avoid moving around or pacing up and down. This can be quite distracting for the audience

Finally, attempt to enjoy it! Remember that most people in the audience are likely to have been in your place at some time or another and realise how far out of the comfort zone doing a presentation can be.

Chapter summary

This chapter identified the anxieties associated with doing a presentation. It provided useful tips and techniques to reduce your stress levels as well. These included:

✓ The daily thought record – a tool to help illicit and rate unhelpful thoughts, which can then be rephrased to be more helpful

✓ Coping imagery – a technique where you imagine yourself in the stressful situation, but imagine that you are coping with it

✓ Practical tips – ideas on how to prepare your presentation, including advice on visual aids, the structure of the presentation and your delivery

Learning points from the chapter

Use the space provided opposite to note down any techniques or comments you found useful in this chapter.

Helpful resources

Presentation Skills for Students. Becker, L. and Van Emden, J. (2004). Basingstoke: Palgrave Macmillan.
A practical, accessible guide for all students in further or higher education. It discusses speaking effectively in seminars, tutorials and formal presentations, and helps with career research.

14

Preparing for exams

What this chapter covers

This chapter explores the reasons why you may find exams stressful. It highlights the common barriers to effective exam revision (e.g. time management, procrastination, excessive anxiety and additional responsibilities). This section also covers effective exam techniques which include timetabling, memory aids, maintaining a healthy body and mind, challenging negative thinking and how to prepare for the day of the exam.

Why do we become stressed about exams?

Exams are generally stressful for most of us because they are one off assessments which require our best possible performance on the day. Most topics that have been covered during the course are tested, under tight time constraints, and it is under standable that many students worry whether they can do themselves full justice under exam conditions.

In addition, personal or family expectations about exam performance can trigger stress, as can the need to acquire certain grades to be successful in further studies or to enter into certain professions.

Whatever the reasons, the outcome is the same – if your stress levels become too high over a prolonged period of time it can be detrimental to your chances of exam success and even to your general health.

As mentioned in Chapter 2, the right amount of pressure is good for you. By using techniques and preparing for exams in advance, you can turn stress and excess anxiety to your advantage by channelling that energy to perform at your peak.

Common barriers to effective exam revision

Time management

Being effective in managing your time enables you to make the most of your revision as well as giving you some time to relax and wind down. There are a number of factors which may hinder effective time management, such as not having a clear idea of how long each topic will take to revise, leading to your scheduled free time being swallowed up by extra revision, and the most common of them all … avoidance of the task or procrastination (look at Chapter 12 for more detail).

Procrastination

Do you ever find that when you sit down to study, you remember a 101 other things that need doing? Maybe you have to call your family or you notice how dirty your room looks? It's amazing how many chores that go unnoticed for such a long time become urgent and in need of immediate attention as soon as there is exam revision to do. We often avoid work that we are anxious about doing, but this behaviour only exacerbates our levels of stress rather than reducing them in the long run. Remember, you procrastinate to get a quick stress-reduction fix! But it doesn't last for long.

Many students explain the avoidance of exam revision as being due to a heightened ability to perform well under pressure: *'But I work best in the eleventh hour'*. Although, many of us believe we produce our best work when burning the candle at both ends, leaving your revision until the last minute seldom increases your effectiveness. Usually a person puts themselves under so much unnecessary pressure they tend to make mistakes. Also, at the eleventh hour no time is left for problems such as mislaid notes and crashing computers. This, coupled with a lack of sleep, which reduce your levels of concentration, is the perfect recipe for heightened levels of stress on the day of your exam.

Excessive anxiety

As mentioned previously, for most people exams equal pressure and stress. Although a little tension is natural and to be expected, it is when you begin to feel overwhelmed by the prospect of exams that this can lead to depression or anxiety. It is important to remember that no matter how nervous you are of taking exams or how worried you are about failing, you can get help – there is no reason for you to be stressing on your own! Although no one can sit the exams for you, you can get helpful advice from friends, family, lecturers or other students or from counselling centres. If you would prefer to speak to someone who is completely objective, there are a number of support groups and organisations which are qualified to help listed in Appendix 2.

Panic attacks

Another form of anxiety which can sometimes take a student by surprise is the onset of panic attacks. Panic attacks affect around one in every 75 people, and they usually appear during teens or early adulthood. Although the exact cause for the onset of the attacks is unclear, there does seem to be a connection with life transitions, which are viewed as being particularly stressful. Panic attacks can be terrifying as they appear to arise out of nowhere and occur even in seemingly harmless situations, such as when you are sleeping. Whilst it is important to note that panic attacks are not dangerous, they can be frightening because youfeel so *out of control*.

The main symptoms of a panic attack include:

- Chest pains or feeling as though you may choke
- Intense feelings of terror and fear
- Racing heartbeat
- Breathing difficulties – feeling as though you can't breathe or can't get enough air
- Trembling, sweating, shaking
- Pins and needles in hands and feet
- Dizziness, light-headedness or nausea
- Fear of death (many people believe they are experiencing a heart attack)

Sufferers of panic attacks often find it useful to repeat coping statements such as:

'This is only a panic attack, this will gradually peak and then die down again, just like all the other ones have done. It is not a heart attack.'

'I really don't like this panic attack but I've stood it before and I'll stand it again.'

'Just because it feels really bad, it is not awful. I've survived them before.'

Using statements such as these help you to keep the panic attack in perspective and to remind yourself that you are not about to die of a heart attack. Writing a coping statement on a small card can be quite useful. Keep the card in a handy place such as your wallet or purse so you can read it as soon as you are becoming panicky.

You may recall that in Chapter 13 we recommended completing a daily thought record to help you deal with stress. Many people find completing these forms helpful in dealing with panic attacks too as they can be used to challenge your unhelpful and negative anxiety-provoking thoughts. A completed daily thought record focusing on John's panic attacks is illustrated below.

Panic attack sufferers may also find it useful to practise breathing techniques (see Chapter 4 for more details) to calm themselves down.

Case study John's daily thought record for panic attacks

Situation	Unhelpful thoughts	Emotions	Helpful response
1. Describe actual event leading up to unpleasant emotion or 2. Stream of thoughts, daydreams or memories 3. Distressing physical sensations	1. Write down any thought(s) that came into your head before the emotion(s) 2. Rate your belief in automatic thought(s) from 0–100%	1. Specify the emotion you feel – are you anxious, angry, sad and so on? 2. Rate the degree of the emotion you feel 0–100	1. Write down a helpful response to counter the unhelpful thought(s) 2. Rate your belief in the new helpful response 0–100% 3. Re-rate emotions 0–100
Palpitations, breathing quickly, feeling faint, tingling sensations	*This feels terrible (95%)*	*High anxiety (90)*	*This feels bad but it is not the end of the world (75%)*
	I'm going to die (90%)	*Panic (100)*	*Panics have not killed me before! I hate this feeling but I'm not dying (90%)*
	I can't breathe properly (90%)	*High anxiety (95)*	*Calm down. Just focus on breathing slowing through my nose. I am still breathing (70%)* *I now feel only 45 on my anxiety scale*

Please note: if you believe you may be suffering from panic attacks please consult your GP or the university medical centre for a proper diagnosis.* The good news is that if it is dealt with promptly by a qualified cognitive-behavioural therapist, medication will probably be unnecessary. (See list of useful organisations and websites at the end of the chapter.)

*Cognitive-behavioural forms of therapy are recommended by the National Institute for Health and Clinical Excellence to help deal with anxiety, phobias and panic attacks. There is plenty of published research demonstrating its effectiveness with these problems. Be careful when looking at other forms of therapy or counselling – the therapist should be able to show you how it will help specifically with panic attacks. A focus on your childhood problems probably won't help you to tackle your current panics. It is worth noting that in this book we have taken a cognitive approach to dealing with stress.

Additional responsibilities

For some students, the stress of exams can be exacerbated by other responsibilities, such as being a carer or parent, or having financial commitments requiring you to continue working whilst studying (see Chapter 17 for more information). Additional commitments require some students to manage their time better than other students and to be more disciplined.

However, if the situation becomes too difficult, or you feel you are unable to manage juggling all your commitments, help is often at hand and universities are generally very understanding. In these situations, a discussion with your lecturer or tutor can lead to a more manageable arrangement which can relieve some of the pressure.

Effective revision techniques

Structuring the time available

To manage your revision effectively you need to be aware of how you are allocating your time. When beginning revision it is imperative that all revision topics are looked at in detail, to see what areas will need more revision time and what areas can be covered in a shorter period of time. It is also useful to revise the difficult areas first, or those topics that you don't really want to do or are attempting to avoid. This will free up more time closer to the exams to be revising topics which you enjoy or find easier.

Having a revision timetable

As mentioned in Chapter 12, the best way of organising all the topics and areas for exams is in a revision timetable. This does not have to be a piece of artwork (this would be an example of further procrastination!), but a clear table, indicating realistic study periods which are linked to your exam dates.

It is a good idea to prepare a timetable fairly early on, as this will assist you in visualising what needs to be done before the exams. To re-iterate, the main points to remember when creating a revision timetable are:

- Be realistic. If you are a morning person, timetable most of your revision for that time of the day
- Vary the topics to maintain your concentration
- Ensure you allocate time for meals and relaxation
- Don't entirely cut down on free time for relaxing, socialising or exercise – they are important too and time out helps you to approach your work afresh

Example Revision Timetable

EXAMS MINUS FOUR WEEKS

Morning	Exam 1 – reading lecture notes	Exam 3 – reading notes	Exam 1 – further reading	Exam 2 – further reading	Exam 3 – further reading	DAY OFF	Lie in
Afternoon	Exam 1 – preliminary notes/mind maps/spider diagrams	Exam 2 – preliminary notes/mind maps etc	Squash and out for light lunch	Exam 4 – sorting out lecture notes/getting all up to date	Exam 2 – condense further reading with notes/mind maps	DAY OFF	Exam 3 – condense further reading with notes/mind maps
Evening	Exam 2 – reading lecture notes	Going out!	Exam 3 – preliminary notes/mind maps	Exam 1 – condense further reading with notes/mind maps	Exam 4 – reading lecture notes	DAY OFF	Go through course syllabus – need to cover all topics

EXAMS MINUS TWO WEEKS

Morning	Exam 2 – consolidate notes	Exam 1 – use techniques to assist revision/learning	Exam 4 – consolidate notes	Exam 3 – consolidate notes	Exam 1 – practice paper	Exam 3 – revise/learn	Exam 1 – consolidate notes/learning
Afternoon	Exam 3 – consolidate notes	BREAK	Exam 4 – use techniques to revise	Exam 1 – use techniques to assist revision/learning	BREAK	Exam 2 – revise/learn	Exam 1 – revise/learn
Evening	Exam 2 – use techniques to assist revision/learning	Exam 2 – revise/learn	Exam 4 – Meeting study group to go through tips and ideas	Gym	Exam 3 – use techniques to assist revision/learn	BREAK	Exam 1 – Meet study group to go through tips and ideas

EXAMS MINUS ONE WEEK

Morning		Exam 1 – practice paper	Exam 3 – consolidate final notes	Exam 2 – revise/learn	Exam 3 – revise/learn	Exam 4 – revision/learn	Exam 3 – final revision
Afternoon	Exam 2 – revise/learn: get any questions for group	Exam 2 – consolidate final notes	Exam 1 – revise/learn	Exam 2 – practice paper	Exam 3 – practice paper	Exam 4 – practice paper	Exam 2 – final revision
Evening	Meet study group to go through tips and ideas for Exam 2	Exam 1 – consolidate final notes	Exam 2 – consolidate final notes	Gym	Exam 1 – final revision	BREAK	BREAK

Memory aids

We tend to be more receptive to new facts and figures if they are presented to us in different ways. Nowadays there are lots of different memory tools to help us remember, without learning things parrot fashion. However, learning how to use the varying techniques one week before the exams is probably not a good idea. Most of the techniques do require time and practice, so get a basic understanding of them early on. Once you have grasped the key elements of the techniques you will be well equipped with skills to help you revise more effectively.

Using mnemonics

- Rhyme – '*In fourteen hundred and ninety two, Columbus sailed the ocean blue*'
- Acronyms – An abbreviation formed from the initial letters of a series of words, such as the BBC (British Broadcasting Corporation) or NUS (National Union of Students). Acronyms are even more effective if they actually spell a word. For example, if you need to remember the three types of mnemonic mentioned in this section (Rhyme, Acronyms and Mapping), then the word RAM could be used to denote the first letter of each word.
- Mapping or spider diagrams – Spider diagrams are good for making notes round a central topic. They are also useful for generating ideas for essays, whilst mind maps are an extension of spider diagrams and can help to organise topics both visually and linguistically.

Being organised

This may seem like quite an obvious suggestion, but being organised assists in helping you to revise smart not hard! In addition, you reduce the last-minute tension which often arises when you are disorganised, allowing you more time to prepare without increasing your stress levels.

Get hold of the course syllabus as this will alert you to any gaps in your notes or areas where you may need further information. It will also help you, before the revision really gets started, to catch up on any notes you may have missed. Find out about any resources that are available, whether they are in the guise of internet sites or revision guides: they are there to help so should shed light on possible examination areas.

One of the most helpful resources is to get hold of previous exam papers. These are invaluable for preparing for the forthcoming exam. Working through examples and previous papers will give you a good indication of what topics may be more likely to come up, the style of questions asked and the time available in which to answer them. Along with previous papers, and wherever available, examiners' notes regarding past exams can be very useful as they indicate what examiners like in a model answer and it also highlights what their pet hates are!

Avoiding temptation

As mentioned earlier, procrastination increases your stress levels. In addition, it is the main culprit for not sticking to your revision timetable. For these reasons, minimise the risk of temptation by limiting the number of attractive alternatives to studying available in your immediate environment. Work in a place where you are least likely to be disturbed or contacted by friends. Libraries are normally a good place, although it can sometimes be difficult to refrain from meeting up with friends at the library and spending most of your time 'on breaks'.

'I used to arrange to meet up with my friends on a particular floor of the university library, which was great initially when I didn't have much to do. But it soon became a meeting point making it difficult to get any work done there. When it was exam time I actually ended up studying on a different floor from my friends so that I could get some studying done! The library was also the place where I checked my emails, so when I was busy I had to make a specific effort to check it only when I arrived and when I left the library.'

Alex, 30 years, London

Keeping mobile phones or landlines off when you are studying will also prevent distractions. These precautions are particularly useful when you are practising exam papers under timed conditions or learning new material.

Maintaining a healthy body and mind

During exam periods, staying healthy and fit has a very positive impact on the mind and reduces the impact of stress on your body. Exercise is a fantastic way to relax and relieve stress, because it promotes a greater sense of well-being and alleviates physical tension and feelings of lethargy. This has the knock-on effect of helping you feel fresher and more energised. It is also good for people who have sleeping difficulties around exam time, as moderate exercise will help to take your mind off problems and stress.

Hand in hand with exercise goes diet. A good diet full of nutrients will help your brain stay alert and active. Reducing your intake of fizzy drinks, tea and coffee may also make a difference, as caffeine is known to over-stimulate the body, often resulting in an inability to sleep or ineffective study. Over-indulgence can also make you feel sluggish and drowsy, so you are likely to be less productive after your meal. The aim should be to follow a balanced and nutritional diet.

Having enough sleep is also essential to effective revision. Everyone needs different amounts of sleep, but ensure you have at least six to eight hours sleep a night. It is unlikely that you will be taking in much information if you are tired.

Challenging negative thinking

As mentioned earlier, exams bring with them pressure and expectations. No matter how much of a positive thinker you are, sometimes unhelpful thoughts such as '*what if I fail*?', may cross your mind. This is perfectly natural and it is good to think of this eventuality so that you are prepared for all outcomes. However, if you find that you are beginning to obsess over the thought, or you are trying to convince yourself of inevitable failure, it is necessary for you to face these thoughts and challenge them.

Although we have covered a number of different types of negative thinking in Chapter 3, it may be useful to go through some more specific fears relating directly to exams. The table below lists a few unhelpful thoughts that you may have. If you have any others add them to the list and think how you can challenge that negative thought or fear and come up with a more positive and effective approach.

Problem: Possible negative thoughts during exam time

Stress-inducing thinking (SIT)	**Stress-alleviating thinking (SAT)**
• I'm no good in exams, I'm much better in coursework	• Although I prefer coursework, if I prepare myself (timed exams etc), it will be like doing a piece of coursework quickly
• There is no point revising for this, I'm going to fail anyway!	• If I don't revise soon I will definitely fail, but if I put in some hard work now, I might just pass so it's worth giving it a go
• What will I do if I fail?	• If I fail, there are plenty of opportunities for me to retake or re-think what I would like to do instead
• What will people think of me if I fail?	• What do I think of people who have failed in the past? I don't think negatively about them, so they will probably understand too
• How will I tell my parents/guardian if I fail?	• I can only do my best and they will commiserate with me. But there's no point talking like I've failed already – I'll give it my best shot!
• I have no choice – I must pass this exam	• It would be strongly preferable to pass these exams, but there is no law stating that I must. I will do my best
• Any other negative SITs?	• Any other SATs?

© 2005 Centre for Stress Management

It is important to understand that although you may have little or no control over certain aspects of the exams, such as what questions they ask, you do have control over the way you perceive the stress of exams and how you choose to respond to it. It is helpful to consciously listen to any negative comments that you express and note how they affect you. By doing this, it is easier to learn to rephrase your thoughts in a way that will be more motivating and helpful. For example, many of us may, at some time in our lives, have felt that we have left studying until the last minute: *'There is only two days till the exams – there is no way I can get through all of the topics left!'*

Whilst it may be true that you don't have enough time, thinking along these lines conjures up feelings of helplessness, fear and panic. It would, for example, be more useful to say to yourself: *'I know I can't cover it all, but I do have time to cover the most important topics, so lets concentrate on that.'*

This will help you to stay in control of the situation. Remember to focus on what you can do rather than concentrate on what you can't. Remember, too, it is only with a positive frame of mind that you work at your best.

De-stressing during the exam period

Here are some of the main ways to maintain an inner sense of calm during the exam period. This is by no means an exhaustive list, but it aims to remind you that during the exam period it is important to take some time out to relax both your body and mind.

- **Breathing exercises** – These simple techniques can be done anywhere, are easy to follow and have been found to reduce symptoms of stress, leaving individuals feeling energised and uplifted. Examples of deep breathing and meditation techniques can be found in Chapter 4.
- **Maintaining your routine** – Everyone has different daily rituals that they enjoy. These may include your first cup of tea of the day, listening to music or watching television. In addition, many of us have *'stability zones'* (Palmer, 1989), which may incorporate some of your daily routines. These stability zones are physical areas where you feel safe and relaxed, such as having a bath, playing music loud in your room, or reading in bed. These are usually different for different people, but they are all habits which make you feel more relaxed. During exam periods, you may find that you are *too busy* or feel too guilty to indulge in these routines as you feel you have not got enough time (for example, not watching your favourite TV programme because you feel that you may be wasting valuable revision time).

  However, it has been shown that maintaining these routines (in moderation!) act as a stress buffer, helping you to cope better with pressure. It is interesting to note that although humans are creatures of habit, when you are under stress and pressure, you often change your routines. This self-sacrificing behaviour is often not that fruitful and is unlikely to make you feel any better.

- **Activity** – Staying active during the exam period alleviates lethargy and helps concentration. Even for those of you that do not '*do*' exercise, a 20-minute brisk walk will make a notable difference to your outlook when you return to the books.
- **Take time-out** – Making sure you allocate specific slots for recreation gives you time to unwind and take your mind off your work. These breaks from work should be planned and timetabled to prevent anxiety or feelings of guilt. Negative thoughts, such as '*I don't have time for this*', can then be countered with '*I have stuck to my timetable, and this evening/time is my reward for doing what I had set out to do today*'.
- **Support groups/revision groups** – Having a network of friends or colleagues to support you around the exam period can act as a buffer against stress. Groups can be used to discuss issues or problems that you may be facing. They may also provide solace that you are not the only one feeling a particular way and they may help to keep your thoughts and emotions in perspective.

Revision tips

There are a number of ways to keep on top of your revision. Aids and techniques are plentiful and it is important to find the ones that are most effective for you fairly early on in the revision process. Many students find a variety of different techniques are useful, depending on the type of exam being taken, for example, multiple-choice or short-answer questions, essays, aural or practical exams. Outlined below is a brief summary of generic revision tips.

✓ Avoid longs spells of just reading notes – not only is it hard work and time-consuming, but after a certain amount of time you may just '*switch off*'

✓ Take breaks – remember your attention span only lasts between 40–60 minutes. Take regular breaks to keep yourself alert

✓ Set up a routine so you revise at the same time each day – consistency actually helps the memory processes

✓ Revise your weakest subjects or those you absolutely hate first, as you will probably need to do extra revision for them. It is no good putting these off because when you eventually do come to them, you may be tired and less inclined to put in the required amount of study time

✓ When writing summaries of topics, try to present material in different ways, such as mind maps or spider diagrams, because this is more likely to hold your interest for longer, making it easier for you retain information

✓ Use mnemonics

✓ Prioritise key points from each section of a topic

✓ Mix dull topics with interesting ones. The variety may keep you awake!

✓ Meet up with friends to revise, they may have other ideas and points you have missed

✓ Revise by working through past papers to find out re-occurring questions and model answers

How to prepare on the day of the exam

- **Sleep** – Although you may be anxious, try and get a good night's sleep before an exam. If you have difficulty getting to sleep, try some of the relaxation exercises outlined in Chapter 4.
- **Food** – Eat something before the exam, even if it is a small amount, to help you concentrate. If you are allowed to, take a bottle of water into the exam to keep yourself hydrated.
- **Leave plenty of time to get to the exam** – Make sure you know where the exam is taking place and leave plenty of time to get there. We have all heard stories of students missing their exam, turning up to the wrong exam or in some instances going to the wrong place.

'It was my French aural exam. I went to the room where it was supposed to be, knocked on the door, and entered ... it was a store room!!! I had written the room number down incorrectly. So I spent the next 15 minutes in a frantic panic trying to find out which room I was supposed to be in!'

Christina, 19 years, Leicester

- **Before entering the exam room** – There is always nervous chatter when waiting to enter the exam room. If you find that talking to people makes you feel more apprehensive or nervous, the best approach is avoid people and spend the time on your own, maintaining a sense of calm.

When in the exam room

- Take time to read each question carefully and tick the questions which you feel you would like to complete first.
- A commonly mentioned tip is to read the questions carefully and answer the question asked – not the one that you may have revised for!

- On a rough piece of paper, write a quick plan (bullet points will do) of how you are going to answer each question. This will help you to give a structured and methodical response.
- If you are running out of time on a particular question, write a skeleton argument, noting down the key points which you would have expanded on. This should pick you up some marks.
- Make sure you attempt all questions. If you don't know the answer … just guess! You might be lucky.

Chapter summary

This chapter looked at common barriers to effective revision and discussed methods to overcome procrastination, excessive anxiety (including panic attacks) and negative thinking. It also highlighted skills and techniques to reduce stress levels during this highly pressurised period of time. These techniques included:

✓ Time management skills

✓ Use of memory aids such as mnemonics

✓ Stress-inducing thoughts and stress-alleviating thoughts forms (SITs versus SATs)

This chapter also included useful tips on how to revise and prepare on the actual day of the exam.

Learning points from the chapter

If you have found any of the techniques in this chapter helpful for reducing your stress levels, use the space provided below to note them down.

Helpful resources

Association for Rational Emotive Behaviour Therapy
PO Box 8103, Colchester, Essex CO5 9WL
Tel/fax: 01376 572 777 (general enquiries)
Website: www.arebt.org

Provides a list of accredited therapists who deal with stress, anxiety, phobias, panic attacks and depression using rational emotive and cognitive-behavioural therapies.

British Association of Behavioural and Cognitive Psychotherapies
The Globe Centre, PO Box 9, Accrington BB5 0BX
Tel: 01254 875277
Fax: 01254 239114
Email: babcp@babcp.com
Website: www.babcp.org

Provides a list of accredited therapists who deal with stress, anxiety, phobias, panic attacks and depression using cognitive-behaviour therapies.

British Association for Counselling and Psychotherapy
1 Regent Place, Warwickshire CV21 2PJ
Information telephone line: 01788 578328
Website: www.bacp.co.uk

Provides a list of accredited counsellors and relevant organisations.

Centre for Stress Management
156 Westcombe Hill, London SE3 7DH
Tel: 020 8293 4114
Website: www.managingstress.com

Provides online self-help material, counselling, coaching and training.

Make Exams Easy: Learn Time-proven Exam Techniques, Boost Your Confidence and Results, Understand what Examiners Look For. **Evans, M. (2000). Oxford: How To Books**
The book gives advice on achieving success in exams and covers a set of critical tools, techniques and approaches which aim to boost skills

and confidence. It includes guidance on key preparation, planning and revision methods which can be applied to all levels of exams.

How to Pass Exams: Accelerate Your Learning, Memorise Key Facts, Revise Effectively. O'Brien, D. (2003). London: Duncan Baird Publishers.
The book outlines the steps you can take to increase your memory power and pass your exams. *How to Pass Exams* will show you the easy way to accelerated learning and help you achieve top grades in any subject using a number of innovative techniques.

Part 5   Coping with university

In Part 5 of the handbook we begin by exploring student relationships at university. Chapter 15 covers all aspects of relationships, from finding a partner to splitting up. Advice and techniques to assist you through each of the various stages are illustrated throughout.

Alcohol and drugs are addressed in Chapter 16. As there is plenty of literature on the dangers of drugs and alcohol available from your university and the web, this chapter focuses on the effects that different drugs have, how to identify whether you have an alcohol or drug problem and assertion skills to remind you that you have the right to say *no* if you want to.

Even though universities are fairly cosmopolitan, incorporating people from all walks of life, some groups of students may find it harder to adapt to university than others. In Chapter 17 we explore reasons why some students may feel out of place and discuss ways in which these concerns can be addressed.

15
Relationships

What is covered in this chapter
Relationships can be a major cause of pressure and stress at university. This chapter takes a brief look at the types of relationships at university (from non-committal one nighters to longer-term relationships). It also looks at how to deal with conflict in a relationship, including information on effective communication techniques, such as assertion skills and the empty chair technique.

Finding a partner

'The main reason why I chose this university was because of the degree course, but of course I checked out the male: female ratio just out of curiosity!'

Noel, 19 years, Brighton

University is a fantastic place to meet people and it is unlikely that you will ever find so many opportunities to get together with people you are attracted to. That does not mean that you *should* find a partner, or even expect to find your perfect dream relationship within the first few weeks of being there.

Looking at current trends from the *Student Experience Report 2005* (MORI, 2005), it appears that nearly a quarter of students are already in serious relationships (24 per cent), whilst a further 13 per cent are living with someone or are married. This means that just under half of all students are single (49 per cent) and most of them are happy to be so (63 per cent)!

'I'm single and I plan to stay that way for quite some time. I'm not saying I don't want fun with guys ... but serious relationships are something I want to steer way clear of!'

Ellen, 18 years, Oxford

Sex

With nearly half of the student population being single at university, sex is often on the agenda! Whether you are into one-night stands, drunken mistakes or having a bit of fun, if you are planning on having sex on a night out, use a condom! Condoms and other contraceptives protect you against sexually transmitted diseases, HIV and unwanted pregnancies. Research also indicates that if you are under the influence of alcohol or drugs, there is a higher risk of you having unprotected sex. So, don't let a good night out get spoilt by a careless mistake. Take precautions!

Getting pregnant

One in six female students has had a pregnancy scare after having unprotected sex. Evriwoman survey (NOP, 2003)

The risks of pregnancy after unprotected sex are fairly high and the stress that can result from this is even greater! In all the excitement of leaving home, meeting new people and enjoying your newly found freedom, contraception may not be on your list of priorities:

'I went out clubbing with a few friends and I got chatting to this guy at the bar. I hadn't planned for a big night out ... anyway, when we got back to my place things started heating up. ... I know this sounds stupid, but I was too embarrassed to mention using a condom! I know, it sounds really pathetic now, I don't know, maybe I thought it would kill the mood – I guess I just wasn't thinking straight. You're not really thinking about the consequences at the time!'

Nicole, 18 years, Exeter

Talking about contraception with your partner can feel awkward and embarrassing, so it is worth thinking about how you would deal with a similar scenario to Nicole's, or how you would discuss it with your partner before the mood takes you. The assertion and communication skills outlined in Chapter 5 may help.

However, if you do find that you are pregnant, act quickly and seek advice on what your options are as soon as you can. Your student health care centre should be able to offer you non-judgemental advice on what choices are available to you.

Alternatively, if you would like to discuss your pregnancy with an independent agency, there are a number of organisations which can offer you support and information during this stressful time. A list of services and websites you can contact are available at the end of this chapter and in Appendix 2 of the handbook.

Exploring your sexuality

University is also an excellent time to explore and become more confident with your own sexuality. It is a time of self-discovery, and it is not surprising that gays and lesbians often find themselves coming out at university (this is discussed in more detail in Chapter 17). There are numerous activities, organisations and societies which help you to be open with your feelings and sexuality. However, if you are confused about your sexuality or would like to talk to someone in confidence, you can contact your student counselling services or contact support organisations which will be able to give you further guidance and information.

Relationship problems

When you are in love, life is a breeze and you are flying high, but when you stumble across relationship problems, everything can appear to be crashing down around you. This can put you under immense pressure and impact on your physical well-being as well affecting your academic work.

Whether you feel you are constantly arguing or on the verge of breaking up, the emotional upset can be overwhelming. The causes for disputes or stress in a relationship can occur for a variety of reasons, from incompatibility, lack of communication, financial difficulties to illnesses.

One of the first steps of dealing with problems in a relationship is identifying what is going wrong:

- Are you too busy with your own sets of friends to make time for each other?
- Are you talking to each other enough?
- Have you become more short tempered and impatient with your partner?
- Do you feel restricted by having a partner in your new surroundings?
- Have you found someone else?
- Is your partner making you feel jealous?
- Are you being yourself around your partner?

Once you have identified possible reasons for your behaviour towards each other, it is easier to find techniques to deal with it.

Express yourself!

One of the problems frequently mentioned among couples is that they don't talk enough about the important things. People often keep feelings they find hard to deal with to themselves (such as anger or jealousy). Emotions can then build up to boiling point and can often spill out in a totally inappropriate setting or over something completely unrelated. Below are techniques which can help you to express your emotions in a more constructive way.

Its not you, it's just your behaviour!

As discussed in Chapter 3, when we are under pressure we are more likely to rate ourselves or someone else more negatively. This applies to behaviour as well. Think of the last time you were annoyed with your partner. Did you label them as 'a waste of space', 'a loser', or 'useless', or did you stay calm and identify their behaviour as the problem rather than them personally?

'She can't handle her drink, but she is normally okay.'

By diverting your anger to the behaviour as opposed to the person as a whole, you are more likely to lower your levels of stress. It is also more likely that your partner will take on board the mistakes they have made without getting defensive about them.

The empty chair technique

You may not want to tell your mates what you are about to do, but this technique really works when you want to understand what is really bugging you and how you feel about the situation or the person.

Sit in a quiet room at a time when you will not disturbed by others. Place an empty chair opposite you and imagine your partner sitting in it. Think of a conversation that you would like to have with your partner. Be honest and state exactly what you feel and think. Remember, if you are angry with them, stick to what they have done that you dislike (the behaviour), rather than making a statement which puts them down as an individual (a global statement such as 'you're pathetic!'). For example, 'I get annoyed when you don't clean up after yourself' is likely to be received more calmly than 'You are so lazy you don't do anything around the flat'.

You can change seats at any time, or give a response that you think your partner would give whenever you want. Continue the conversation until you begin to see what the main problem or issue appears to be. This will then help to clarify what you want to discuss with your partner.

Communication skills

There are numerous ways of improving communication and dealing with conflict in a relationship. Here are a few quick tips on communicating more effectively:

- Be honest
- Avoid blaming each other. Use 'I' statements as opposed to 'You' when explaining how you feel
- Monologue's are not conducive to resolving problems – make sure you both have a chance to explain your side of the story
- If you have been wrong, accept responsibility for your actions/behaviours
- Give constructive feedback on a person's behaviour. Generalising their actions (e.g. *'you always do this!'*) will only put them on the defensive.

Being assertive

By learning to communicate assertively you are able to express your concerns and worries in a direct and honest way, which reduces stress and misunderstandings (see Chapter 5 for more detail). For example, the de-fogging technique can be very effective when in a heated discussion. It involves picking out the main points which warrant further discussion and ignoring the irrelevant 'put downs' which may arise. This helps to keep the discussion focused on the main issues and allows you to maintain your self-respect.

Partner: *What's wrong with my friends? You never want to come out with us and you always come up with some lame excuse as to why you can't come! It's like you've got this chip on your shoulder – you're too good for them?*

You: *I already had plans for this evening and as far as I'm aware I don't have any issues with your friends.*

Breaking up

Every relationship is not made in heaven. If you are not happy being with someone, it is worth considering why you are still with them. Break-ups are not easy and letting go of someone is tough. Talk to friends and family for advice and if you feel that this is not the relationship for you, be strong and positive about your decision. It may help to use projection imagery (Chapter 4, section 1) by thinking about how you will be managing in six months time from now without your partner, and then whether you will be coping well in a year from now. Imagine how you will have moved on from the relationship over time.

If feasible, surround yourself with friends or family after a break-up for the support and comfort. It may feel difficult now, and you may not want to hear it, but time is a great healer. Breaking up can also be a good way of learning more about yourself, and what you want from any future relationships. University is a fantastic place to meet new people, so don't give up just yet!

Chapter summary

This chapter looked at ways of managing relationships at university and included information on:

✓ Enjoying the opportunities to meet a range of people within the university setting

✓ Precautions to take before having sex

✓ What potential problems may arise in a relationship at university

✓ How to deal with conflict in a relationship – this included effective communication skills and using the empty chair technique

✓ Breaking up with your partner at university

Learning points from the chapter

Use the space provided below to note down any comments or techniques you have found useful in this chapter.

Helpful resources

Family Planning Agency
2–12 Pentonville Road, London N1 9FP
Tel: 0845 310 1334 (9am to 6pm, closed on Thursday
3pm–4.30pm)
Sexual health information line: 0800 567 123
Email: www.fpa.org.uk

Gives confidential information and advice on contraception and
sexual and reproductive health. It also provides details of family
planning clinics, sexual health clinics and other sexual health
services elsewhere in the UK.

Relate
Relationships hotline: 0845 130 4010
Website: www.relate.org.uk

Relate is the UK's largest provider of relationship counselling and
sex therapy. Relate offers advice, relationship counselling, sex
therapy, workshops, mediation, consultations, and support face
to face, by phone and through the website.

British Pregnancy Advisory Service
Helpline: 08457 30 40 30 (action line for unplanned pregnancy)
Website: www.bpas.org

Marie Stopes International
Helpline: 0845 300 8090
Website: www.abortion-help.co.uk

London Lesbian and Gay Switchboard
Tel: 020 7838 7324 (24 hours)
Website: www.llgs.org.uk

A voluntary organisation that aims to provide a 24-hour
telephone and referral service for lesbians and gay men.

16

Alcohol and drugs

What is covered in this chapter

Alcohol and drugs are part and parcel of university life. From Fresher's week all the way to graduation, many an ex-student could spend endless hours reciting stories of alcohol-infused fun and enjoyment. The aim of this chapter is not to lecture on the vices of alcohol and drugs but to highlight potential patterns of behaviour which may lead to alcohol and drugs abuse – when alcohol and drugs are no longer just a 'laugh' or associated with a 'good night out' but are a craving that needs to be fulfilled to get through the day.

The chapter looks at the attraction of drugs and alcohol, their usage levels and the effects of different drugs on your body. It also helps you identify whether you have a drug problem.

Alcohol

The man takes a drink; the drink takes a drink; the drink takes the man. (Old Chinese proverb)

In Britain drinking is a socially accepted habit with no questions asked once you hit the age of 18. Statistics show that 90 per cent of the UK population over the age of 15 drink alcohol on a regular basis. Studies relating to the student population have shown that 10 per cent of students drink to hazardous levels (more than 50 units a week), whilst a third are within the high-risk category (drinking between 20 and 50 units a week). Although it is still early days, there is also growing concern regarding excessive drinking now that the licensing laws have been relaxed. Whatever the impact will be, it is clear that with alcohol being on tap 24 hours a day, there is a greater need for students to take responsibility for the amount of alcohol they consume.

The main problem with excessive drinking is that it promotes tolerance to alcohol, which allows the drinker to drink more alcohol and yet feel less intoxicated. So although you may be one of those people *'who can handle their drink'*, looks can be deceptive. Despite feeling fine, the physical damage to the brain and liver continues, co-ordination is affected and the withdrawal symptoms increase over time.

Alongside the physical damage of drinking, heavy alcohol consumption affects our mental state of mind, which makes us more susceptible to depression and insomnia. Alcohol is also consumed to a greater extent when we are stressed and under pressure, or when we are bored and need something to do.

Another, yet less obvious, side-effect of drinking is putting on weight. Alcohol has a high number of hidden calories, making it very hard to lose weight if you are a heavy drinker. For example, it has been stated one gin and tonic contains the same amount of calories as a bowl of ice cream. So consistent drinking can lead to very noticeable weight gain!

Alcohol Concern also warns us that young people are twice as likely to have unprotected sex under the influence of alcohol. This can have a number of distressing outcomes such as unplanned pregnancies, HIV and other sexually transmitted diseases.

So drinking can have some serious implications but these can be limited by drinking in moderation* and planning ahead for a big night out!

Drugs

Having a joint with a few drinks hardly seems like a big deal, especially when we take into account the usage and acceptance of them in certain environments. Drugs have always been used to celebrate, relax and escape from everyday life. The only difference is that certain groups of people have used them to different levels and extents, and it is this which shapes our laws and beliefs within society.

You may have come across a number of drugs already, such as tobacco, marijuana and cocaine. If you have not already been offered or taken some of these substances, it is likely that you may in the future. It is worth taking some time to explore what you think and feel about the various drugs before such a situation arises. There is so much information available over the World Wide Web and from your own university that it is fairly easy to find out all there is to know about literally every drug in existence. By being equipped with all the knowledge about what particular drugs do and the effects they may have, you will be in a much better position to make an informed decision on whether you want to take a drug or not.

Drugs are very powerful substances, and one of the greatest concerns with drug taking is the temptation to over-indulge. However, there is no real classification of

---

*The recommended guidelines set by the Department of Health are 3–4 units of alcohol a day for men and 2–3 units of alcohol per day for woman. However, many health professionals still recommend the previous guidelines of a maximum of 21 units a week for men and 14 units a week for women.

what constitutes an unhealthy level of usage. This is because the effect of a drug varies greatly depending on the drug being used, the amount taken and the user's experience with the drug. In addition, the environment in which it is used and the mental state of the user also impacts on the effects. To complicate things even further, an individual can have a different effect from the same drug at a different time of usage. So it is wise to exercise caution as drugs are powerfully addictive, whether the dependence is physical or psychological.

But experimentation is part of life. Research indicates that 41 per cent of students admit to taking some form of illegal drugs, with 39 per cent having taken marijuana, one in ten ecstasy and one in twelve (8 per cent) cocaine (MORI, 2003). However, it is not usually experimentation that creates problems for the individual but it is the repeated use, coupled with the illegality of some drugs that put you at risk.

The attraction of drugs and alcohol

I want to drink poisons, to lose myself in dreams and visions.
(IHCOYC XPICTOC)

People take drugs* for all sorts of reasons. For many it starts off being experimental, and a bit of fun. Peer pressure also appears to be a major factor.

'I remember my first time. We were at a house party when one of my mates took out some tablets (speed). He said it would be a bit of a laugh and keep us going all night. Everyone else took one, so it didn't look like such a risky thing to do'.

John, 18 years, Nottingham

A number of students also believe that drugs and alcohol will make them more relaxed and a bit more confident. Drugs are often taken in a group setting, which can give you a feeling of group belonging and a feeling of commonality with the other users. In addition, different drugs have different effects, which add to the experimental aspects of drug taking. For example, some drugs are taken for their transcendental affects (LSD), whereby they distort reality and can cause hallucinations, whilst other drugs, such as speed or cocaine, can make the user feel very energetic.

---

*For the remainder of the chapter, drugs will refer to both illegal street drugs as well as more mainstream drugs such as alcohol and tobacco.

Yet drugs are not just taken when people are feeling good; drugs are also used when people are feeling low. With many drugs (including alcohol), they are used as a 'pick me up' or to help people forget about their problems. For the time it's being taken, an individual's insecurities may feel as if they disappear, taking the edge off a situation and making it more bearable for them. This is when taking drugs can have the worst outcomes. Drugs start being used to forget or consistently to give an *added extra*. The drugs stops being used for recreational purposes and starts to be a necessity for the individual.

The effects of drugs

There is no one particular way that people will react to drugs, simply because everyone is different and each drug impacts on an individual in different ways. If you do decide to experiment with drugs, remember:

- One person's experience will not necessarily mirror the experience you will have
- No two experiences are necessarily going to be the same even if the same drug is taken

The effect a drug will have on you will depend on your mood, who you are with and the atmosphere of the place you are in. So it is important for you to decide what you want to take. Do not rely on other people's experiences – do your own research.

'I had known this guy for a couple of months and went round to see him one evening. He offered me an acid tab and I thought – why not! They say that if you are in an unfamiliar place or with someone you don't know that well, it can play on your insecurities ... well that's what happened to me. A little while after I took it, I started getting paranoid about my friend's intentions. Soon his face started distorting – and he turned into a lion! I was shit scared. He kept coming over to check on me, which freaked me out even more. I have never touched it since.'

Alfie, 18 years, London

Know your drugs

Alcohol

Found in drinks like beer, lager, Alco pops, cider, wine and spirits.

The effects
- Many people enjoy drinking alcohol and in small amounts it can help people to feel more relaxed and sociable
- Some people can use alcohol to escape from their problems
- The effect depends on the strength of the drink and how fast it is consumed
- The effect also varies according to when a person last ate, what their weight is, their mood and surroundings
- Speech can become slurred, co-ordination is affected and emotions are heightened
- A hangover can leave you feeling ill for a day or so

The risks
- Alcohol is a depressant drug and users can end up feeling very down
- Women get more drunk than men on the same amount of alcohol. They can also develop drink-related health problems earlier in life
- Drinking too much alcohol can lead to a loss of consciousness. Users then risk choking on their own vomit. This can kill
- Overdosing can also cause alcoholic poisoning, which can be fatal
- Long-term overuse can lead to serious liver, heart and stomach problems
- More than 25,000 deaths in the UK each year are alcohol-related
- Mixing alcohol with other drugs is seriously dangerous!

Anabolic steroids

Trade names include: Sustanon 250, Deca-Durabolin, Dianabol, Anavar and Standzolol, some users may refer to them as 'roids'. Anabolic steroids can only be sold lawfully by a pharmacist to someone with a doctor's prescription. Whilst possession is not illegal, even without a prescription, supply is against the law and C penalties apply (14 years in prison and/or a fine).

Anabolic steroids are similar to, and include, the male hormone testosterone. They are used in medicine to treat anaemia and muscle weakness after surgery, they are not the type of steroids used to treat eczema/asthma. It can be swallowed although most of them need to be injected. Some body-builders and athletes use anabolic steroids, as do people who think it will improve their body image. However, its use in sports is prohibited and a positive test for the drug can ruin a sporting career.

The effects
- Users claim steroids make them feel more aggressive and able to train harder
- With exercise, anabolic steroids can help build up muscle. However, there is some debate about whether they improve muscle power and athletic performance
- They help users to recover from strenuous exercise

The risks
- Taking anabolic steroids carries many health risks and can stop young people from growing properly
- The risks for **men** include: erection problems, breast growth, shrinking testicles, reduced sperm and even sterility, acne, an increased a chance of heart attack and liver failure
- The risks for **women** include: growth of facial hair, deepening voice, shrinking breasts, irregular menstrual cycle, spots, possible miscarriage and stillbirth if pregnant
- Some effects, such as the change in breast size, may be irreversible without surgery
- Injecting into veins can be dangerous and injecting into muscle can damage nerves and veins. Sharing needles or syringes puts users at risk of dangerous infections like hepatitis and HIV

Cannabis
Other names that it goes by include marijuana, draw, blow, weed, puff, shit, hash and ganja.

Cannabis is a natural substance and is derived from the 'Cannabis Sativa' plant, commonly called *hemp*. It comes in a solid dark lump known as resin, or as leaves, stalks and seeds called *grass* or sometimes as a sticky oil. It can be rolled with tobacco in a spliff or joint, smoked on its own in a special pipe, or eaten. There are different strengths of cannabis – some, such as skunk, are very strong.

Cannabis is a Class C drug, with the maximum penalty for possession being 2 years in prison and/or a fine and for supply it is 14 years in prison and/or a fine

The effects
- Getting stoned on cannabis makes most users relaxed and talkative
- It heightens the senses, especially when it comes to colours, taste and music
- Cooking and eating hash makes the effects more intense and harder to control
- It can leave people feeling tired and lacking energy
- Hash may bring on cravings for certain foods

The risks
- It affects short-term memory and your ability to concentrate
- Getting stoned affects co-ordination, increasing the risk of accidents
- It impairs driving skills, so it's not advisable to get in the car and drive or be driven by someone who is stoned
- It can make users paranoid and anxious, depending on their mood and situation
- Smoking joints with tobacco can lead to users getting hooked to cigarettes
- Smoking cannabis over a long period of time may increase the risk of respiratory disorders, including lung cancer
- Many users find cannabis hard to quit

Cocaine

Other names used to refer to cocaine include coke, Charlie, snow and C.

Cocaine is a white powder that can be snorted up the nose or injected. It is a class A drug so the maximum penalty for possession is 7 years in prison and/or a fine, whilst supply of cocaine can lead to life imprisonment and/or a fine.

The effects
- Cocaine is a powerful stimulant and the buzz creates a sense of well being, making the users feel alert and confident
- The effects last about 30 minutes
- Users are often left craving for more
- People may also take more to delay the comedown (which includes tiredness and depression)

The risks
- Cocaine can cause heart problems and chest pain
- Heavy use of cocaine can cause convulsions
- Large or frequent doses over a short period of time can leave users restless, confused and paranoid
- Snorting cocaine can permanently damage the inside of the nose
- Users may find their habit expensive and hard to control
- Users have died from overdose

Crack

Alternatively known as rock, wash or stone. Crack is a smokeable form of cocaine and is also a Class A drug, with the same maximum penalty as Cocaine (possession – 7 years in prison and/or a fine; supply – life imprisonment and/or a fine).

The effects
- The effects of smoking crack are similar to snorting cocaine but much more intense
- The high lasts as little as 10 minutes
- Users often *chase* the high by repeating the dose
- Heavy users make take heroin to dull the craving caused by the use of crack

The risks
- Heavy use can lead to potentially fatal heart problems
- Heavy users risk convulsions
- Crack is highly addictive and because the high can be so intense, crack use is difficult to control

- Smoking crack can seriously harm the lungs and cause chest pains
- After the high, feelings of restlessness, nausea and sleeplessness are common
- Large or frequent doses over a short period can leave users restless, confused and paranoid
- Regular users may find their habit very expensive
- Users have died from overdose

Ecstasy

Other common names for it include E, Fantasy, Doves, Mitsubishis, Dolphins, Rolexes. Its chemical name is MDMA.

Ecstasy usually comes in a tablet form of different shapes, size and colour, but is often white. The effect MDMA will have on an individual is often unpredictable, especially as a tablet may not contain MDMA. However, some are sold as MDMA and can have very different effects.

Ecstasy is a class A drug, so carries a maximum of 7 years in prison for possession and/or a fine, and a maximum of life imprisonment and/or a fine for supplying the drug.

The effects
- Users can feel alert and in tune with their surrounding and other people
- Sound, colour and emotions can seem much more intense
- The energy buzz from ecstasy means that users can dance for hours
- The effects can last anything from three to six hours

The risks
- As ecstasy starts working (known as *coming up*), users may feel a tightening of the jaw, nausea, sweating and an increase in heart rate
- The comedown can leave users feeling tired and depressed, often for days
- Use has been linked to liver and kidney problems
- Studies into the effects of ecstasy are still at an early stage. However, research shows that MDMA dramatically affects the brain chemistry of animals
- There have been about 60 ecstasy-related deaths in the UK

Please Note: As ecstasy affects the body's temperature control, dancing for long periods in a hot atmosphere increases the chances of users overheating and dehydrating. These risks can be minimised if users:

- rest at regular intervals
- sip about a pint of non-alcoholic fluid such as fruit juice, isotonic sports drinks or water every hour

Gases, glues and aerosols

These are sniffed or breathed into the lungs.

The effects
- Users feel thick-headed, dizzy, giggly and dreamy
- It can be hallucinogenic
- The effects disappear after 15–45 minutes
- Afterwards, users may feel drowsy and may suffer from a headache

The risks
- Use of gases, glues or aerosols can cause instant death – even on the first go
- Squirting the products down the throat may cause the body to produce fluid that floods the lungs. This can be fatal
- Abusing gases, glues or aerosols can lead to nausea, vomiting, black-outs and fatal heart problems
- Accidents can occur when the user is high because their senses are affected
- There is a risk of suffocation if the substance is inhaled from a plastic bag over the head
- Long-term abuse can damage the brain, liver and kidneys

Please note: Sniffing gases, glues or aerosols kills one person every week

GHB

This is sometimes known as GBH, and is short for gammahydroxybutyrate.

It is a colourless liquid and is sold in small bottles or in capsules. The liquid is measured out in capfuls and then swallowed. It has no smell but has a salty taste. GHB is used as an alternative to anabolic steroids.

GHB is a Class C drug carrying a maximum penalty of 2 years in prison and/or a fine for possession and 14 years and/or a fine for supply.

The effects
- GHB has sedative properties and can produce a feeling of euphoria
- The effects have been known to last a day

The risks
- Excessive hits could lead to sickness, stiff muscles, fits and even collapse
- If incorrectly produced, GHB can badly burn the mouth
- It is very dangerous and can be fatal when mixed with alcohol or other drugs
- The long-term effects of GHB are not yet fully known

Heroin

Otherwise known as Smack, Brown, Gear, Horse, H, Junk, Skag or Jack.

Heroin is a painkilling drug made from morphine, which is derived from the opium poppy. It comes in the form of a white powder when pure. Street heroin is usually brownish-white. It is snorted, smoked or injected.

It is a Class A drug carrying the maximum penalty (possession – 7 years in prison and/or a fine; supply – life imprisonment and/or a fine)

The effects
- In small doses, heroin gives the user a sense of warmth and well-being
- Higher doses can make them drowsy and relaxed
- Excessive amounts can result in overdose, coma and in some cases death
- First-time use often leads to side-effects like dizziness and vomiting

The risks
- Heroin is very addictive. Getting the next fix can dominate a user's life
- Tolerance develops, which means the user needs more heroin to get the same effect
- Users who form a habit may end up taking the drug just to feel normal
- Those who start by smoking or snorting heroin sometimes switch to injecting to maximise the high
- Injecting can damage veins and lead to gangrene
- Sharing needles or syringes puts users at risk of dangerous infections like hepatitis and HIV
- Withdrawing from heroin can be very hard
- Many people do manage to wean themselves off heroin although mentally it can take years before you are completely free of it

Ketamine

Also known as Special K, Vitamin K or just K.

Ketamine is an anaesthetic with painkilling and psychedelic properties. It comes in tablet form or as a powder snorted up the nose. Ketamine is a prescription-only medicine. Although possession is not illegal without a prescription, supply is against the law.

The effects
- It makes users feel that the mind has been separated from the body. This creates *out of body* and hallucinatory experiences for up to three hours
- Like LSD, the effects are influenced by the user's mood and environment. In some instances a user may be physically unable to move

The risks
- As ketamine numbs the body, users risk serious injury without feeling the pain
- The effects can be quite alarming if the user isn't expecting them
- Excessive doses carry some risk of breathing problems and heart failure
- Ketamine is very dangerous when mixed with alcohol and other drugs
- The long-term effects of recreational use of ketamine are still not really known

LSD (Acid)

Other names include: Trips, Tabs, Blotters, Microdots and Dots. Its chemical name is Lysergic acid diethylamide.

LSD usually comes in tiny squares of paper often with a picture displayed on one side. The picture has no relevance to the effect or strength of the drug.

LSD is a Class A drug carrying the maximum penalty (possession – 7 years in prison and/or a fine; supply – life imprisonment and/or a fine)

The effects
- LSD is an hallucinogenic drug which has powerful effects on the mind
- The effects of LSD are known as a *trip* and can last as long as 8–12 hours. Whilst a user is tripping they will experience their surroundings in a very different way
- The effects depend on the user's mood, where they are and who they are with
- Sense of movement and time may speed up or slow down. Objects, colour and sound may become distorted
- Users experience trips differently every time

The risks
- Once the trip starts, there is no way of stopping it
- A bad trip can be terrifying. Users may feel very threatened and can even forget that the drug is responsible
- It is impossible to predict a bad trip, but it is more likely to happen if the user is feeling anxious, nervous or uncomfortable
- Feeling paranoid or out of control can leave users shaken for a long time afterwards
- Accidents may happen whilst users are hallucinating
- Users may experience flashbacks, where parts of a trip are briefly re-lived some time after the event
- LSD can complicate mental problems such as depression, anxiety and schizophrenia

Magic mushrooms

…Or 'shrooms and mushies. There are several types of magic mushrooms that grow wild in the UK. The main type is the Liberty Cap mushroom. However, there are two species that look similar to magic mushrooms but which are poisonous. Magic mushrooms are eaten raw, dried, cooked in food or stewed into a tea.

Although it is not illegal to possess raw magic mushrooms, it is an offence to possess any preparation of them (e.g. when they're dried or stewed). Magic mushrooms when prepared are Class A drugs. The maximum penalty for possession is 7 years in prison and/or a fine, and for supply is life imprisonment and/or a fine.

The effects
- Magic mushrooms have a similar affect to LSD, but the trip is often milder and shorter
- Magic mushrooms can make users feel very relaxed and 'spaced out'. The effects depend on the user's mood, where they are and who they are with
- They may cause hallucinations – objects, colour and sound become distorted
- A trip tends to last about four hours

The risks
- Magic mushrooms often cause stomach pains, sickness and diarrhoea
- Eating the wrong kind of mushroom can also cause serious illness and even fatal poisoning
- If users feel sick, they should go straight to hospital with a sample of the mushroom and explain what has happened
- Bad trips do happen and can be very frightening. Once the trip has started, there is no going back
- Like any hallucinogen, magic mushrooms can complicate mental problems

Poppers (or alkyl nitrites)

Trade names include: Ram, Thrust, Rock Hard, Kix, TNT and Liquid Gold.

Poppers is a term used for the group of chemicals known as alkyl nitrites. Poppers come as a clear or straw-coloured liquid in a small bottle or tube. The vapour is breathed in through the mouth or nose. Over recent years the use of poppers has become more common, especially in the dance culture. Amyl nitrite is prescription-only medicine and although possession in not illegal, supply can be an offence.

The effects
- Users get a very brief but intense *head rush*. This is caused by a sudden surge of blood through the heart and brain. Blood vessels enlarge, resulting in a flushed face and neck

- Some users say that they experience the impression of time slowing down
- The effects fade 2–5 minutes after use

The risks
- It can make some people feel faint and sick, especially when taken whilst dancing
- Users often experience a headache afterwards
- Regular use causes skin problems around the mouth and nose
- Taking alkyl nitrites is very dangerous for people with anaemia, glaucoma and breathing or heart problems
- If spilled, poppers can burn skin
- Poppers may be fatal if swallowed

Speed (amphetamines)

Other names include: Whiz, Uppers, Amph, Billy and Sulphate.

Speed is usually a grey, white or dirty white powder, or sometimes it is in tablet form. It can be snorted, swallowed, injected or smoked. Speed is the most impure illegal drug in the UK.

Amphetamines are Class B drugs but carry Class A penalties if they are prepared for injection. The maximum penalty for possession is 5 years in prison and/or a fine, and for supply is 14 years in prison and/or a fine.

The effects
- Speed is a stimulant; it quickens the heartbeat and breathing rate
- Users may feel confident
- Minds may race and the user may feel energetic
- It suppresses the appetite but does not satisfy the body's need for nourishment
- Some people also become tense and experience feelings of anxiety

The risks
- The comedown (tiredness and depression) lasts for one or two days and some-times longer
- Sleep, memory and concentration are all affected in the short term
- High doses repeated over a few days may cause panic and hallucinations
- Long-term users may become dependent on the buzz speed gives them
- Tolerance can develop, which means the user needs more to get the same effect
- Long-term use puts a strain on the heart. Overdose can be fatal
- Use of speed can lead to mental illness such as psychosis

Tobacco

Tobacco contains a drug called nicotine, which is very addictive.

The effects
- Nicotine is a powerful and fast-acting drug
- When smoke is inhaled the nicotine effect hits the brain about 8 seconds later
- Nicotine speeds up the heart rate and increases blood pressure
- First-time users may feel sick

The risks
- It is very easy to get hooked
- Smoking is expensive. Ten cigarettes a day will cost upwards of £500 a year
- Tobacco smoke contains over 4000 chemicals, many of which are harmful to health
- Smokers are more likely to suffer coughs and chest problems. A long-term tobacco habit can lead to cancer, emphysema and heart disease – all of which can kill
- Passive smoking can cause breathing difficulties, asthma and even cancer
- Tobacco contributes to at least 2000 limb amputations and 111,000 premature deaths in the UK each year

(Information on knowing your drugs is reproduced from *The Score: Facts about Drugs*, published by the Department of Health (2004)).

How do you know that you have a problem?

Many people experiment with drugs and many either stop after a while or become recreational users. Unfortunately, this pattern of behaviour is not universal, alcohol and drug abuse can just sneak up on you. From being a recreational user, one can slip into a cycle of dependency. Nobody plans to do this, and many individuals are not even aware when it occurs. For this reason, it is good to keep a check of your drug habit so you are aware of when you may be becoming a bit extreme. The following set of questions can be used as a checklist:

- Do you have a favourite drug you use?
- Do you ever use drugs when you are alone?
- Do you use drugs because you are bored, lonely or anxious?
- Do you think a lot about drugs and drug use?
- Do you plan your day to make sure you can use drugs?
- Do you need to use more and more drugs to get the effect you want?

- Do you feel irritable or anxious if you do not get to use drugs?
- Do you miss your favourite drug if you do not use it for a while?

The more 'yes' answers you give, the more likely it is that your drug use may have become excessive. It is worthwhile reassessing your level of drug intake and pattern of usage to maintain control for yourself.

Drugs help some people to cope with stress and this can sometimes lead to them becoming reliant on them. It is also worth remembering that when you are stressed you are more likely to take more drugs or consume more alcohol which has serious implications for your health. If you feel that you may benefit from professional help and guidance, refer to 'Helpful resources' at the end of the chapter or go to Appendix 2 of the handbook for a list of services and helplines you can contact.

Know your limit – get assertive!

Whether you experiment with drugs or not is your choice, so it is important that you are taking drugs for the right reasons. That is, because you want to, and not because of peer pressure.

However, one of the biggest problems with just saying *no* is that it is not always that simple! Being the sensible voice of reason and caution in many ways can be badly received by your new experimenting friends. So how do you keep your friends and make the choice that's right for you? By being honest with yourself and by being assertive!

Assertion is a fantastic skill that can be used in many tricky situations. It's basically the skill of getting the balance between being a complete push over and being a ranting preacher. Being assertive puts you back in control and makes sure you do what is best for you.

Assertion is said to be linked into one's own levels of self-esteem. People with lower self-esteem and feelings of self-worth are less likely to state what they honestly feel and may end up resentfully following the crowd. However, an assertive individual is likely to be more confident and have a higher level of self-worth as they are more in control of what they want to do.

Assertion is something which takes time and practice to acquire, but remember you have the right to:

- say no
- to consider your own needs as being important
- to take responsibility for your own actions
- to do what you feel is right for you

Acting assertively helps you to maintain your rights and give you the confidence to do what is right for you. An example of assertion is illustrated in the model below.

The three-step model

This model can be used in any situation, but especially if you are feeling intimidated or under pressure to comply to other people's demands. Using this model you can make your point in an assertive manner, without offending and, more importantly, without drifting off the point you want to make or becoming emotional.

Step 1 – Actively listen to what the other person is saying and demonstrate to the other individual that you have heard and understood what they have said.

Step 2 – Say what you think and feel (a good linking word to use between steps 1 and 2 is 'however').

Step 3 – Say what you want to happen (a good linking word to use between steps 2 and 3 is 'and').

Using the same peer pressure example as above, the technique can be used in the following way:

Step 1 – *Okay I get the point. If we are all tripping it will make the evening more of a laugh.*

Step 2 – *However, I'm too much of a control freak to give it a go.*

Step 3 – *And so I think I'll give it a miss this time.*

For more information on assertion techniques look at Chapter 5, section 1.

Chapter summary

Taking drugs is a choice, so it's important that it is *your* choice. The aim of this chapter was not to condone the activity of drug taking, but to provide you with information on the following aspects of drug use:

✓   The effects of drugs and alcohol

✓   Awareness of when you may be over-indulging

✓   The effects of drugs

✓   Assertion techniques to use when you know your limit

Learning points from the chapter

Use the space provided below to note down anything you have found useful in this chapter.

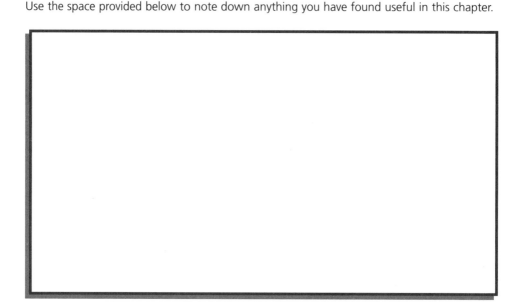

Helpful resources

Alcohol Concern

Waterbridge House, 32–36 Loman Street, London SE1 0EE
Helpline: 020 7922 8667 (Monday–Friday 1pm–5pm)
Email: contact@alcoholconcern.org.co.uk
Website: www.alcoholconcern.org.co.uk

Gives information, guidance and advice for those worried about their own drinking habits or somebody else's. It also contains publications and a directory of local alcohol services.

Alcoholics Anonymous

PO Box 1, Stonebow House, Stonebow, York YO1 7NJ
Helpline: 0845 769 7555 (24-hour service, calls charged at local rates, calls are redirected automatically to an AA member in your region)
Email: aanewcomer@runbox.com
Website: www.alcoholics-anonymous.org.uk

FRANK

Helpline: 0800 77 66 00 (24-hour service)

Text phone: 0800 917 8765

Email: frank@talktofrank.com

Website: www.talktofrank.com

Offers free and confidential advice about any drug issue, whether it is information you require, advice or a chat. The website also contains facts, guidance and support information.

17

Feeling out of place?

What this chapter covers

The word 'student' often evokes the image of a young carefree individual. Even though universities have gone to great lengths to incorporate people from all walks of life, you may still sometimes feel isolated and different from your fellow students. Whether it is due to people's attitudes, falling out with friends or not enjoying your course, being at university can sometimes feel very lonely.

This chapter deals with the specific issues which may confront particular groups of students in a university setting. These include:

* Being a mature student
* Living at home
* Students with disabilities
* Gay and lesbian students
* Having caring responsibilities
* Students from overseas
* Practising your faith

Issues that are covered include finances, juggling commitments, dealing with conflict (anti-guilt imagery and step-up techniques are used), isolation, and adjusting to university life.

What do you want from university?

For many students feeling homesick or isolated becomes less intense as time goes by. You make friends with like-minded people, gain a greater understanding of your environment and the way things work at university and create your own support networks and daily routines.

Nevertheless, first-year students are not a homogeneous group. Students come from all walks of life, from different age groups, different countries and of course with different expectations of the university experience:

'I'm here to meet new people, have a great time! Oh yeah ... and obviously to study!'

Daniela, 18 years, London

'To get a better job when I leave uni – I think it will enhance my career prospects.'

Ian, 19 years, Cardiff

'I have always had an interest in the arts, so I'm here to get a greater understanding and basically enjoy what I am learning. So no I don't have any other expectations of university as such, well other than to learn!'

Margaret, 45 years, London

'I needed to get a degree to secure a better job in the market place.'

Tanya, 28 years, Middlesex

'Having a good education from overseas, puts me in a good position when I go back home. I'm here to work hard, play hard and to get the good grades.'

Ashish, 22 years, Newcastle

This chapter will focus on certain groups of students who have additional responsibilities or pressures which may impact on their adjustment to university life. By emphasising these groups of students we are not suggesting that these students find university life any easier or harder than the rest of the student population. However, it is likely that many of these students have experiences and concerns which make their adjustment to university life different from that of other students.

Being a mature student

'I just felt so old when I walked into the student canteen! I thought being a mature student may make me feel a bit out of place, but I had no idea! I looked as though I was one of the lecturers not a student, I was so self-conscious! Also I think the label of being a mature student doesn't help – when you think of mature, you think of old, sensible and boring!!! But it is amazing how you get used to things. I don't even notice the differences

that much now. I'm obviously at a loss with some conversations that my friends have, but they usually explain what they are talking about! You have to get on with it, and once you do, you can have just as good a time as the next person.'

Franc, 35 years, Leicester

Anyone over the age of 21 is classified as being a mature student. There is no evidence that mature students enjoy university any less than their younger counterparts. However, if you find that you are having difficulty coping with the adjustment to university life, here are commonly raised problems and possible ways of dealing with them.

Learning to learn again

Depending on how long it has been since you have undertaken formal studies, some students find that their study skills are a little rusty or they feel they are not as good as they would like them to be. In addition, some mature students may feel slightly inadequate when compared to the younger undergraduates who have been through the schooling system for an uninterrupted period, and who appear to be at ease with computers, email and technology as a whole! There are usually two possible explanations for these concerns. The first is a need to update your study skills so they assist you on your course and the second is your confidence in your own abilities and skills. So what can you do about it?

Be proactive – If you genuinely feel that you do need more help with study skills, find out what is available at the university. Many universities run a wide range of study classes to help students with note taking, essay writing and revision techniques alongside courses to get your internet skills and computer skills up to date. Alternatively, you can get some good self-help study resources from the library. There is an enormous selection of good books to help you with your techniques and to help you produce good quality work.

Compare your work with that of your fellow students to check whether you are covering the correct points. However, if you are really concerned, talk to you tutor and/or lecturers about your concerns. A good way of seeing how you are progressing is to ask for feedback from assignments. This will highlight any possible weaknesses to improve upon, but also put your mind at rest, as it is likely that you have been more worried about it than the problem warranted.

Do a reality check – There is no evidence proving that mature students are less effective or do not get the same good grades as their younger counterparts, so it is worth asking yourself why you are questioning your abilities – is it fear or fact? It is often the case that insecurities come into play, especially when there is no evidence to back up your beliefs. It may be worth remembering that you were accepted on to the course, so the university believes that you are good enough to be here. So why don't you?

Finance

It is likely that becoming a student will impact on your financial status. For example you may have worked previously and are now coping without an income. You may also find that you have to cut down on certain expenses due to the costs of being a student and having a more limited income. Forward planning and budgeting your finances is key to helping your money last throughout the term time.

Depending on your circumstances, you may be entitled to financial support. You will need to contact your local education authority (LEA) for a full assessment of the help that the government can give you. For an indication of what you may be entitled to, you can always check the Department for Education Skills (DfEs) website: www.dfes.gov.uk/studentsupport

You may also be eligible for additional financial help from your university (such as Access to Learning Fund, Awards or Hardship funds which some universities provide). It is worth contacting your student services to find out what financial support you are eligible for.

Socialising

Getting to know other students can be just as overwhelming for a mature student as for younger students. Concerns about whether people will like you, whether they will think you are too old, or worrying about how to start a conversation with someone else is natural. But the thing to remember is that everyone is in the same boat.

'Everyone is meeting everyone for the first time. Forget about whether they will like you or not – just let it happen.'

Adi, 24 years, Norwich

Some mature students may find that they have limited time for socialising, especially if they have other commitments outside university. This can make it fairly difficult to break into groups or circles of friends that have already begun to form outside the lecture room. This is also why many mature students seek each other out. They are likely to understand the lack of time they have for socialising and may share similar backgrounds and experiences.

'Most of the friends I made were mature students or students that lived at home. Simply because they hadn't formed stronger relationships with the other students who had gone out clubbing or lived together in halls. I don't think I missed out though. I had a strong

social network outside university, so I didn't need that kind of intense socialising. I set up study groups and did meet some great people. It was just the out of hours socialising I couldn't manage!'

Jodie, 25 years, London

In some instances, being a mature student may create a few barriers to socialising with other students, but they are not impossible to overcome. Although you may not be able to go out every night, that doesn't mean you have to stop completely.

'I just tell the guys if you're planning a night locally around town – don't forget me! They know to give me lots of advance warning too, so I can arrange a baby sitter. I end up going out with my uni lot about once a month. It takes a bit of planning, but it's worth it!'

Sara, 31 years, Kingston

Juggling your commitments and enjoying the university experience

Often mature students have a number of other commitments and responsibilities when they go to university, such as childcare, holding down a job or being a carer. These additional responsibilities can increase the amount of pressure on a student and how one copes varies from person to person.

'I was 11 years old when my father died and I was doing my A Levels when my mum passed away. I've got a sister who is six years younger than me that I look after now. I started university about five years later than I had originally planned because of all the changes that happened at home. When I started university, although I wasn't that much older than most of the other students, I think I had done a lot of growing up over the past few years. My reasons for being at university were very one-dimensional – I needed to get a degree to secure a better job in the market place. I didn't want my sister to struggle the way I did. I didn't really think about socialising with the other students and as time went on I didn't really fit in with any of the other students. So, I would attend my

classes and then just leave. Even if I wasn't working, I wanted to get back home. I don't think I enjoyed university that much, but I think it's true to say, I didn't let myself.'

Tanya, 28 years, Middlesex

Cases like Tanya's are not uncommon, many students end up juggling a number of responsibilities and end up feeling that they do not have the time to make the most of the whole university experience. If you are aware of the responsibilities and pressure that are likely to affect you during term time, it is important to consider what could be done to help you deal with the situations. This forward planning can help you prioritise, manage expectations of the people around you, and also give you time to do what you would like. One way of helping you to clarify what your main priorities and objectives are is to stay focused on them.

Staying focused

When life gets busy, it's sometimes hard to remember what we are trying to achieve. This is often more noticeable when there are lots of demands on our time and we feel under pressure.

The technique below is an imagery exercise. By following the exercise and practising it regularly, you will remember what you want and are more likely to stay focused on achieving it.

Staying focused (or Goal) imagery*

Think of your main priorities or goals. This can be a mix of short-, medium- and long-term aims or objectives. Make sure that they are both realistic and practical for you to achieve. Write them down.

Now for each of the goals that you have written down, imagine a picture or an image that you associate with it.

Practise this imagery regularly (maybe once a day). This will help you to remember what your main goals are and will also keep you focused on obtaining them.

---

*Staying focused imagery was developed at the Centre for Coaching in London by Stephen Palmer.

Case Study **Staying focused**

Tony is a 35 year-old IT student. After a career in teaching English, Tony decided that he wanted to do something completely different. He is married and has one son called Chris who is now 7 years old. Over the last year, Tony has found it harder to deal with all his responsibilities effectively. With his studies getting more demanding, he has also found both his wife and child appear to be needing more of his attention too. He finds himself running around, achieving little and getting frustrated and anxious about completing his work. Tony practised the focus imagery to help him clarify what the most important targets and objectives were.

Short-term goals

1. To get my essay completed within the next two weeks
2. To spend some quality time alone with my wife

Middle-term goals

1. To help Chris learn his part in the school play
2. To finish decorating the spare room

Long-term goals

1. To get a 2:1 in my degree
2. To find a decent paying job in IT
3. To settle down and buy my own flat

Tony then visualised a picture of all his aims. They are outlined below:

Short-term goals

1. To get my essay completed within the next two weeks: *being able to clear my table of all the books and paper relating to the essay topic.*
2. To spend some quality time alone with my wife: *having a candle-lit dinner in a nice restaurant.*

Middle-term goals

1. To help Chris learn his part in the school play: *seeing Chris on stage looking down at me with a big cheesy grin, having said his lines.*
2. To finish decorating the spare room: *clean, blue walls.*

Long-term goals

1. To get a 2:1 in my degree: *a tacky graduation photo of me!*
2. To find a decent paying job in IT: *me on my computer, eagerly tapping away at the keyboard.*
3. To settle down and buy my own flat: *a flat in the centre of town with the lounge having a panoramic view of the city.*

Living at home

Just under a quarter of students (23 per cent) live at home with their parents and family. The main reasons given by students for choosing to live at home is to save money (56 per cent) and one in three believe they cannot afford to move away from home to study (MORI, 2005).

Socialising

As with mature students, living at home, away from the other students, may mean you miss out on some of the nights of debauchery, especially during the first few weeks of university. During Freshers Week making friends may feel slightly harder, especially as many friendships form whilst in halls of residence or living with housemates.

'At the beginning I found it really hard. Everyone would be talking about 'last night' or events that I wouldn't know anything about. I did go out in the evenings but not like them, and it always seemed that something more exciting happened the night I didn't go! Sods law! But once the freshers parties stopped and the humdrum of university life began, I fitted in a lot more. I even think some of my friends actually found it quite refreshing to be around someone who wasn't in their face 24/7!'

Siama, 20 years, Birmingham

Living at home does not necessarily mean the death of socialising. So plan ahead. If your friends are having a big night out on the town, see if you can arrange to stay over at their place or make arrangements for getting home.

With just under a quarter of students living at home with their parents or family, it is unlikely that you are on your own. Making friends with other students who commute to university may prevent feelings of being left out from the wider picture and help you to settle in to your routine more effectively.

Dealing with parental conflict

Parents are often a great source of support, advice and money whilst at university, but inevitably there are likely to be conflicts of interests that arise every now and then. Students who live away from home are not immune from arguments and conflicts with their parents, even if they may be miles away from them – telephones, emails and the occasional visit makes sure of that!

For many students, university means independence and autonomy. However, for students living at home, this may prove to be slightly harder as you're still living in your parents' or family house. Respect for their rules and ways of living may prove to be harder as your lifestyle changes.

It is easy for arguments to escalate into name calling and shouting, and often you may find the heated discussions end up on a completely unrelated topic from the one you were originally discussing (for example, a simple statement like *'can I have some more money?'* ends up being a discussion on the irresponsible and disrespectful youth of the day!).

One way of dealing with conflict is to be assertive. This doesn't mean you tell everyone else the way things are going to be (that would be aggressive behaviour!), but you express your opinion whilst respecting the people around you – without needing to give in to their demands or feelings. It doesn't sound that easy and, to be honest, assertion does need a lot of practice. But the benefits outweigh the effort, as it is a skill that will help you throughout your life (see Chapter 5, section 1).

Finance

Some may say that students living at home have the best of both worlds. You can get to enjoy going out but you don't have the stress of electricity bills, what to eat every meal time and the need to rush to the laundry room before you run out of clothes. Furthermore, with fewer expenses, you may find you have extra cash in your pocket. However, don't forget that this may not always be the case. Additional travelling to get to lectures, costs of lunches at university and the cabs home on nights out may end up eating into your pot of money faster than you think.

Students who live at home do receive a student loan if they are residents of England or Wales. For an assessment, contact your local education authority as soon as possible. The following link will help you locate you LEA contact details: http://www.dfes.gov.uk/studentsupport/students/lea_lea_contact_det.shtml. More information is available in Chapter 11 on Managing your money.

Safety

Although this is a concern for all students, it is a particular concern for students who travel longer distances to and from university. Late night studying or nights out with friends may occasionally mean walking home after dark. Attempt to minimise any potential risks by taking as many precautions as possible. If appropriate, you could invest in a rape alarm, or take self-defence classes if this is something that would interest you.

Students with disabilities

University is a time for change for most freshers. This is no different for a new student with disabilities, especially if specific changes or needs have not been met to enable them to adapt to their new environment.

Under the Disability Discrimination Act (DDA) 1995, your university is obliged to take reasonable steps to ensure that disabled students are not treated less favourably for any reason related to their disability, or placed at a substantial disadvantage compared with non-disabled students. The full Disability Discrimination Act is available at the following link: http://www.legislation.hmso.gov.uk/acts/acts1995/1995050.htm

If you do have a disability, whether it is visible or not, or if you require additional assistance, please ensure that the university is aware of your particular needs as soon as possible. Organise and arrange your requirements early on as this is likely to reduce the stress you may encounter whilst adjusting to university life. It will also make it easier for you to take full advantage of what the university has to offer you.

Finance

Lack of money causes the greatest amount of stress to university students. So, it is worth doing your finances before joining university to ensure that you have budgeted enough money to last you through each term.

Extra financial assistance is also available for disabled students from the government. Depending on the disability, you may be entitled to the Disabled Students' Allowance. This allowance is to help students with the costs they may incur as a direct result of their disability whilst doing their course. Unlike a student loan, the allowance is not dependent on your income or your household income and does not need to be repaid. Depending on your needs, there are four types of financial help available:

- A specialist equipment allowance
- A non-medical helper allowance
- A general disabled student allowance
- Extra travel cost allowance

These allowances are available for both full-time and part-time courses (although part-time students must be studying at least 50 per cent of the full-time course).

You may also be eligible for the Access to Learning Fund. This financial assistance is available through your university.

Support

Having a good support network is an excellent buffer from the stresses and strains that university life may present. Sometimes it can be hard to accept support or tell people that you need help. Research indicates that when under stress, some people actually withdraw from supportive friendships, which prevents them having an outlet to release some of their tension!

'My friends are great but when I went to university I wanted to prove that I was independent and that I could manage on my own even with a disability ... and to a great extent I did. I didn't want my family and friends keeping an eye on me and making sure I was ok. I ended up pushing my best friends and family away from me, because I didn't want them to worry.

Initially adjusting to university was tough. As my disability isn't visible people don't automatically come to your aid — you have to ask! Looking back I guess I just didn't want anyone to know that I was having difficulties. Now I realise how stupid I was being. A lot of people take time to adjust to a new environment, and being disabled I guess I had just that little bit more adjusting to do — it didn't mean I wasn't independent or incapable of looking after myself! If I had let my friends in, I would've probably felt a lot better and less isolated. No one knew what I was like here, whilst my friends could have probably encouraged me and told me how well I was managing. Silly really, I just gave myself a lot of unnecessary tension for nothing!'

Jane, 20 years, London

If you find that you are having difficulty asking for support from friends and colleagues, it may be worth remembering how beneficial supportive relationships are when dealing with stress.

Being able to vent your frustrations or talk about concerns or difficult problems is not a sign of weakness. You would probably expect your friends to come to you if they needed the support, so they are likely to feel the same way too.

Have a go! Support networks

Sometimes it is useful to make a list of friends or family members whom you can turn to, or whom you know will give you good advice. We tend to go to different people for different things, so note down the names of people whom you rely on in the following situations.

- When you have concerns or issues that are worrying you
- When you need someone to calm you down when you are feeling stressed
- When you need to brainstorm or think of a creative way of tackling a situation
- When disaster strikes! When you need someone who can deal with things in a calm and practical way
- When you need a pick-me-up
- When you want to forget about things and have a good laugh

Remember, even if friends are there for you, very few, if any, of them are mind readers! So, unless you tell them they will not necessarily know that you need their help.

Other types of support that are available for disabled students include online resources such as www.skill.org.uk, where you are able to share experiences, keep up-to-date with the law and get up-to-date information on the latest news for disabled people. There are usually informal forums as well, where you can discuss ideas or exchange information with other disabled students.

Exploring your sexual identity

Many students find it easier to explore their sexuality once they join university, especially since the university culture enables students to be more expressive. However, establishing your sexual identity may not be a straightforward process, especially if you feel that being gay, lesbian, bisexual or transsexual may lead to rejection from close friends and loved ones. This can be particularly difficult for students from some communities where they may find that the rejection they face can be community-wide.

'Coming out' is something that most gay and lesbian people face at some point in their lives. How this happens is completely up to you. There isn't one way of doing it. However, you should be comfortable with your own sexuality before telling others.

Who you tell is, again, your decision. Many students have found that telling a close friend or sibling is a good place to start. You are likely to have a good idea of how they will react, even if they are shocked or a little taken back initially (especially if you have known them for a long time and they haven't suspected). Siblings can also be a great help when, and if, you decide to tell your parents. They are likely to have a better understanding of the issues and the family dynamics, so if you have them on your side they may be able to talk to your parents if you don't feel able to.

Telling your parents can be quite daunting, especially if you are worried about how they will react. You may find that they already had their suspicions or that they are completely dumbfounded because it never occurred to them that your sexuality could differ from theirs. Be prepared for difficult questions, stereotyping or awkward questions about your sex life. For more information on coming out, have a look at the list of online brochures available at: http://www.outproud.org/brochures.html

Remember that coming out can be one of the hardest things you may ever have to do. But once you have told your loved ones about your sexuality you are likely to feel relieved and finally be able to move on, in the knowledge that your sexual identity is no longer a secret.

Dealing with disapproval

Coming to terms with your own sexuality can be difficult, so it is worth taking your time before telling other people. One of the biggest fears about coming out is that it may not be acceptable to your close family and friends. It is for this reason that many students keep their true sexual identity hidden for so long. One way of dealing with the fear is to imagine the worst possible outcome of telling your friends and family. This can be done using the Step-up Imagery Technique (Lazarus, 1984).

Step-up Imagery Technique

Imagine a future event that you are anxious about, for example, telling your parents that you are gay.

Step up the picture and imagine the worst possible outcome. For example, being thrown out of the house by your parents.

Now that you have stepped up the image, imagine coping and surviving with that situation. For example, staying over at supportive friend's house until the situation calms down or finding your own accommodation. Practise this imagery regularly until you feel more comfortable with the worst possible outcome. This imagery helps you to then tackle any of the possible scenarios more effectively as you are prepared for the very worst.

Having caring responsibilities

Whether you have children of your own or have adult dependants, going to university with caring responsibilities can be very demanding. Universities generally provide a lot of support for students with these additional responsibilities and it is very important for you to be aware of what support is available and how you can access it.

Finance

Additional financial help is provided by the government for students with caring responsibilities (see Chapter 11). For those with children, these include child tax credit, childcare grant, the parent's learning allowance. For students who have other caring responsibilities there is the Adult Dependants' grant. To find out how much assistance you are eligible for contact your local education authority. Further financial help from your university may also be offered, so contact your local student adviser for more information.

Support

If you have children, your university is likely to provide a level of support for you, such as crèche facilities during university hours. However, many students suggest that support from family and friends was the most important factor for helping them get through university.

'I don't know how I did it. Jake was only one years old when I went to university. I have never needed so much support, discipline and stamina in my life! Childcare was the biggest concern and obviously with a limited supply of money, I needed all the friends and relatives I could get. My mum was great; she would take Jake for an hour or two twice a week so I could get some studying done. She normally looked after Jake when I had lectures too. I lived at home with my mum – there was no other way I could have afforded it. It also meant that any spare moment I had, I needed to be very productive because otherwise I'd feel guilty that the time I was having for myself was precious time that I had borrowed off someone else – usually my mum's!'

Denise, 21 years, Portsmouth

Having support for going to university from close friends and family can be a great source of strength. However, as Denise mentioned above, it can also bring on feelings of guilt, especially towards people who are giving you the support. You may also feel guilty about leaving your child or dependant, as you no longer have as much time to devote to them as you previously had done. Although this is a natural reaction, guilt does cause more anxiety and pressure. Below is an imagery technique to help you deal with any feelings of guilt that you may have.

Anti-guilt imagery*

First, think of all the events or situations which trigger feelings of guilt for you. For example, shouting at a partner, leaving your child or having to leave your dependant with another carer.

Note down next to each of the events any unhelpful or upsetting beliefs or thoughts that trigger feelings of guilt. For example:

'I shouldn't have acted like that; I'm a useless parent; by going to university I'm being selfish.'

Now develop more helpful beliefs that reduce the feelings of guilt. For example:

'It's preferable that I didn't act the way I did, but I did so I will apologise; I'm trying to better myself so both my child and I can have a better future.'

---

*This technique was developed at the Centre for Stress Management in London.

Picture the event or situation in your mind and repeat your new guilt-reducing beliefs. You may need to repeat the procedure and technique regularly for it to be effective.

Case study **Emma's story**

Emma is 22 years old and lives at home with her mother and father and 9-month old child, Clare. She decided she wanted to go back to education once she had Clare. Her parents are very supportive of her decision and look after Clare whilst Emma pursues her degree course.

Event or situation (causing feelings of guilt)	Unhelpful beliefs (triggering feelings of guilt)	Helpful beliefs (reducing feelings of guilt)
Leaving Clare at home	• I'm a useless parent • I'm putting myself before her • She isn't getting the attention of a father and now she doesn't have her mum around her either!	• I can still make lots of time for her, I'm not at university all the time • It's not forever • I am doing this for both of us
Moving on with my own life	• I'm enjoying my life at the expense of everyone else	• I am doing a degree so I can get a better job. I am enjoying university as well, but that means I'm happier which can't be a bad thing for everyone else
Stopping mum and dad (especially mum) getting on with their lives now that they have Clare to look after	• I'm ruining their plans – they probably thought I'd be on my own feet by now and they could enjoy their own life together again • I don't know when I will be able to support Clare and myself	• Mum and Dad fully supported my decision. If they were not happy to do it, they did not have to agree • I am doing my best to secure a better future for us both; the rest is out my hands
Not being financially independent	• I'm an adult and I still can't look after my own child	• I am taking steps to make myself more financially independent
I shouldn't have quit studying after college – I wouldn't have caused so much trouble	• I took the easy way	• I'm only human and make mistakes like everyone else

Emma practised the imagery every morning when she got up and found that she spent less time feeling anxious and had more energy to get on with her day. She also discussed some of her feelings of guilt with her parents who allayed some of her concerns.

Time management

Having additional responsibilities also means that you need to be more effective with the time you have available. A few tips for making the most of your time are outlined below:

Make a list of your weekly goals and targets, which you can amend daily, and tick off the targets you have completed.

- Add in extra time just to allow for the unexpected.
- Avoid procrastination! Putting off your work will only cause a greater amount of stress later on.
- Do one task at a time.
- Use your assertion skills; if you have put time aside to do a certain task don't be distracted or feel obliged to change your timeframe (unless it's an emergency).
- Let people around you know your plans. This way they will be able to support your timetable and are less likely to put demands on your time when you are under pressure.

Goal-focused imagery (see pages 189–91) is also an effective tool to help you achieve your desired outcomes.

Overseas students

Studying abroad can be a rewarding experience – not only do you broaden your outlook and learn about a different culture, but you are also exposed to more subtle differences. You are more likely to come across different rules, behaviours, expectations, food and language, all of which may be far removed from what you are used to back home. Although these differences can be exciting, it can also be stressful, especially when you find yourself on unfamiliar territory and know that this is to be your home for the next few years.

Culture shock

Sometimes moving abroad to a new place can give our system a bit of a shock. It is perfectly natural to feel a little overwhelmed initially, especially if certain aspects of living in a different country seem strange and unsettling. Some students find themselves homesick for a while, missing their country, their food or the weather! However, this is a normal transitional period. Many overseas students soon settle down and adjust to their new surroundings.

However, some students find it harder than others to settle down. Factors such as language may exacerbate the feelings of loneliness and isolation as well. If these feelings of helplessness and isolation continue, you are more likely to feel greater levels of stress and anxiety. Ultimately, this can lead to depression.

'It was a big and very expensive decision to study abroad. My parents spent a lot of money to send me here. But to be perfectly honest, I don't think I knew what to expect. I remember the day I arrived — it was cold and miserable and I couldn't understand a word anyone said — the Mancunian accent just baffled me! I stayed in my room dreading to go out. I hated the weather. I had a few bad experiences with the people in my student accommodation and I wanted to go home so badly. I missed the friendly faces, my mom's cooking and my own bed! I used to cry myself to sleep sometimes — I couldn't even tell my parents I wanted to leave, especially after all the expense! It took me a trip home over the Christmas break to become more settled. Seeing mom and dad made me realise that nothing had changed, and this arrangement was not forever. This gave me great comfort. When I came back to the UK, I was more positive, confident and I made more of an effort to go out with friends. I realised that it wasn't that bad and actually I was missing out on lots of fun things by just sitting in my room being miserable. Yes, it was just different but it didn't mean it wasn't good — but I still hate this weather!'

Abhilashah, 21 years, Manchester

Many students do not necessarily recognise when they are becoming depressed. It can be a slow downwards spiral or you can fall into sets of behaviours. Check the following list of symptoms which characterise people who are suffering from stress and depression:

- Change in appetite; significant weight loss or gain
- Change in sleeping patterns; sleeping too much, unable to sleep or waking up early in the morning
- Loss of interest a;nd pleasure in things you formerly enjoyed doing
- Lethargic, feeling tired all the time
- Feelings of worthlessness or hopelessness
- Feelings of inappropriate guilt
- Inability to concentrate
- Recurring thoughts of death or suicide
- Withdrawing from social interaction
- Physical symptoms such as headaches or stomach aches

Not everyone who is depressed experiences every symptom, and the severity of symptoms will vary with each individual case of depression. However, it is important that if you are feeling isolated or depressed that you contact the university counselling service or inform family and friends and seek professional help.

Practising your faith

Universities are home to a diverse community of people of different faiths, as well as incorporating many who are not practising members of any religion. However, if you are practising a faith, there will be facilities at your university to assist you in doing so. Most universities have a chapel, a prayer room and other such facilities. If you have any particular concerns or requirements, contact your student adviser for more information.

Research has indicated that being part of a religious community can actually help people to deal with stress and other problems more effectively. So it may be worth finding out about religious communities inside and outside the university that may be appropriate for you. There are many religious societies at university which may also help you to find out more information.

'I have made so many friends with other Jewish people through the Jewish Society at university and through the local synagogue. I was worried when I first joined as to how much interaction I would have with other Jewish students, especially as I was such an active member in my own synagogue at home. But having this support of like-minded people has made me less homesick as I feel I have an extended family right here!'

Lisa, 18 years, London

Chapter summary

This chapter explored the potential stressors that particular groups of students may face during their time at university. Issues included finance, having caring responsibilities, isolation and depression as well as safety and conflict. The particular techniques used in this chapter included:

✓ Goal imagery

✓ Anti-guilt imagery

✓ Step-up technique

✓ Prioritising workloads

✓ Being aware of support networks

Learning points from the chapter

If you have any thoughts or comments about this chapter that you would like to note down, you can write them down in the space provided below.

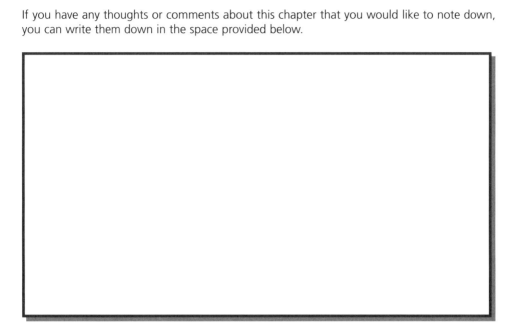

Helpful resources

Outrage!

PO Box 17816, London SW14 8WT
Tel: 020 8240 0222
Website: http://outrage.nabumedia.com

Sexual Health Line

Tel: 0800 567 123 (24 hours)

Gives confidential advice and information about HIV and other sexually transmitted infections. Also provides information on where to find your local sexual health service.

Students with disabilities

SKILL: National Bureau for Students with Disabilities

Chapter House, 18–20 Crucifix Lane, London SE1 3JW
Tel/Minicom: 020 7450 0620

Fax: 020 7450 0650

Email: skill@skill.org.uk

Information service: 0800 328 5050 (freephone) or 020 7657 2337
(ringing on this number saves them money!) – (Tuesdays
11.30am–1.30pm and Thursdays 1.30pm–3.30pm)

Minicom: 0800 068 2422

Email: info@skill.org.uk

Promotes opportunities for young people and adults with any
kind of disability in post-16 education, training and employment
across the UK.

Department for Education and Skills

Link to details about student loans and financial support
available: www.dfes.gov.uk/studentsupport/students/index.shtml

***Learning How to Study Again: A Practical Guide to Study
Skills for Mature Students Returning to Education or
Distance Learning*. Dawson, C. (2004). Oxford: How To
Books.**

This practical book has been written especially for adult
learners, whether they are considering full-time courses,
part-time studies or evening classes. It covers everything you
need to know to succeed in your chosen course, including how
to discover your learning style, improve your reading speed and
memory, take notes and get organised, improve your writing
and mathematical skills, master research techniques, develop
analytical skills and gain marks in exams.

18

University, the Best Time of Your Life?

'Oh yeah, I loved it — had some unreal experiences, met some fantastic people and got a 2:1. I can't complain!'

Roy, 24 years, London

'It was a means to an end — I got my degree and that's what I was there for.'

Tanya, 28 years, Middlesex

'I think it's a bit hyped up! Uni was good but not that good! At least now that I am working, I actually have money to enjoy life without stressing about whether I can afford to go out clubbing AND go to the cinema in the same week!'

Sam, 26 years, Leeds

'The best bit was the complete freedom to do what I wanted when I wanted! I appreciate it more now than I did then — I never realised that it was the only time in my life that I could live the way I wanted with no questions asked. It all changes when you start working!'

Stuart, 23 years, Nottingham

Your university experience is likely to be as unique as you are. How you perceive university will depend on a number of factors, many of which have been mentioned in this handbook.

The underlying beliefs and thoughts that you hold regarding university life will impact on the attitudes you have. In addition, how you handle difficult or stressful situations is also likely to influence your views about university.

Although we hope that your university days live up to your expectations and are relatively stress-free, our good wishes are not enough to ensure that this is the case! This task is in your hands!

Having reached the last chapter of this handbook, we shall now return to the question asked at the beginning – what you were aiming to achieve by reading this handbook. Hopefully, on reflection, many of you have achieved the aims you had set yourself at the beginning. To look at your progress in more detail, let's review what you have learnt over the previous 17 chapters.

Have a go! Revision

Look through the previous chapters and note down any comments you have made in the space provided at the end of each chapter. Also note down any behaviours or attitudes that you identified about yourself from the self-assessment questionnaires that are not very helpful for reducing your stress levels. In addition to this, think of any general areas where you need more practice before you are effective in using them to reduce your levels of stress.

Once you have completed this exercise, you will probably be quite surprised to see how much you have learnt about yourself. It is also quite encouraging to see the number of techniques which are available to help you tackle your stress. There is, however, one more exercise to do before the job of this book is done!

To help you incorporate your new skills into your daily life, you need to plan it in ...

Surviving the stress of university: the self-coaching action plan

Having identified areas for improvement, you can use an action plan to help you focus on the goals that you have set for yourself to survive the stress of university. This can be changed or updated whenever necessary.

To make it easier, the action plan can be broken down into three main areas: psychological, behavioural and physical health. An example of a surviving the stress of university action plan is illustrated below.

Surviving the stress of university: The Self-coaching Action Plan

Action to be taken by: Zara   **Date:** 30 March

1. Psychological

Thinking skills	If I make a mistake I shouldn't be so harsh on myself. I should imagine what I would say to Chris (her best friend), if he had done the same thing.
	I should stop assuming what others think. I am not a mind reader so I need to ask myself what evidence I have before jumping to conclusions!
Imagery skills	When I can't be bothered to do a piece of coursework I can use motivation imagery to remind myself of my ultimate goal – to become a nurse!

2. Behavioural

Social support	Make more of an effort to keep in touch with my friends.
	Remind myself that meeting up with friends keeps me sane! So I should make sure that I keep space in my diary to meet up with my mates at least once a week.
Assertiveness	Keep practising the broken record technique on my mum. This will avoid petty arguments and misunderstandings.
Time management	Stop procrastinating! If I get on with my work, I will have more time to go out later!
	Managing my workload will stop me stressing out last minute when I have more than one assignment to hand in!

3. Physical Health

Exercise	Use the stairs rather than the lift everyday.
	Go to the gym once a week.
Nutrition	Cut down on the chocolate! Stick to one bar of chocolate a day, even if I am feeling stressed!
	Have one spoon of sugar in my tea instead of two.
Relaxation	Make time to relax – fit in yoga once a week.
	Have a bath once a week instead of a shower, will make me feel a bit pampered and will be very relaxing!

207

Have a go! Write your own Self-coaching Action Plan

Surviving the stress of university: The Self-coaching Action Plan

Action to be taken by: **Date:**

1. Psychological	
Thinking skills	
Imagery skills	
2. Behavioural	
Social support	
Assertiveness	
Time management	
3. Physical Health	
Exercise	
Nutrition	
Relaxation	

Keep your action plan in a place where you can see it so you do not forget about it. However, even if you find that you forget to stick to it sometimes, remember it is not the end of the world and start using it again as soon as you can.

Now you are on the way to becoming your own stress coach – congratulations!

The end

Having reached the end of this handbook we hope that you feel better equipped to survive the stress of university and wish you all the very best in your new adventure! If you would like to contact us with your comments and queries or recommendations for the next edition of the book please email us directly: stressguide@managingstress.com

And finally we leave you with a comment made by one of the many people we interviewed whilst writing this book.

'I'd say to anyone joining university – make the most of it! It's a once in a lifetime experience - that time never comes back!'

Sandy, 28 years, Manchester

Appendix 1
Self-hypnosis

Self-hypnosis works by helping you to relax and as you relax you become more receptive to the positive or helpful statements being made, which in the following script asks you to become even more relaxed! Self-hypnosis is not a form of controlling another person's senses or mind. You can either remember the script below or record it on to a tape so you can play it back later. (Important caveat: do *not* practise self-hypnosis on other people unless you are an appropriately qualified therapist!)

When you play the recording back make sure you are sitting in a comfortable chair, preferably with a headrest. Sit with both your hands and legs uncrossed to avoid the possibility of cramp. If you wear contact lenses or glasses, it is advisable for you to remove them before you start the hypnosis.

When reading the hypnosis script, emphasise the word 'down' by saying it slightly louder and by making it last twice as long as usual as this seems to aid relaxation.

> **Please note**: If you have had an unpleasant experience using relaxation or hypnosis on another occasion, then do not use this self-hypnosis script. Do not use it if you have experienced any previous mental health problems or are currently suffering from depression. Do not use it when under the influence of drugs or alcohol. Do not use self-hypnosis when in charge of machinery or driving.

Induction

I'm going to close my eyes *(Pause for 1–3 seconds)*

And now listen to the noises outside the room *(Pause for 1–3 seconds)*

And now listen to the noises inside the room *(Pause for 1–3 seconds)*

These noises will come and go throughout this session and I can choose to let them just drift over my mind or choose to ignore them if I so wish *(Pause for 1–3 seconds)*

(Continued)

(Continued)

I will probably notice how these noises and the sound of my voice will become softer and louder and softer again during this session. This is quite normal and will indicate that I am in a state of hypnosis and relaxation *(Pause for 1–3 seconds)*

My whole body is going limp and slack *(Pause for 1–3 seconds)*

As I keep my eyelids closed and without moving my head, I am going you to look upwards, with my eyes closed, just look upwards *(Pause for 1–3 seconds)*

I can notice the feeling of tiredness and sleepiness … *(Pause for 1–3 seconds)*

And relaxation … *(Pause for 1–3 seconds)*

In my eye muscles … *(Pause for 1–3 seconds)*

And when my eyes feel so tired, so very, very tired, I'll just let my eyes drop back DOWN *(Pause for 1–3 seconds)*

I can notice the feeling of tiredness, sleepiness and relaxation in my eyes *(Pause for 1–3 seconds)*

I'll let this feeling now travel DOWN my face to my jaw *(Pause for 1–3 seconds)*

Now just relax my jaw *(Pause for 1–3 seconds)*

If my teeth are clenched, then I can unclench them *(Pause for 1–3 seconds)*

Now relax my tongue *(Pause for 1–3 seconds)*

I'll let the feeling of relaxation slowly travel up over my face to my forehead *(Pause for 1–3 seconds)*

To the top of my head *(Pause for 1–3 seconds)*

To the back of my head *(Long pause for 5–15 seconds)*

Then slowly DOWN through the neck muscles *(Pause for 1–3 seconds)*

And DOWN to my shoulders *(Long pause for 5–15 seconds)*

Now I am concentrating on relaxing my shoulders, I'll just let them drop DOWN *(Pause for 1–3 seconds)*

(Continued)

(Continued)

Now let that feeling of relaxation now in my shoulders slowly travel DOWN my right arm, DOWN through the muscles, DOWN through my elbow, DOWN through my wrist, DOWN to my hand, right DOWN to my fingertips *(Long pause for 5–15 seconds)*

And I'll let that feeling of relaxation now in my shoulders slowly travel DOWN my chest right DOWN to my stomach *(Pause for 1–3 seconds)*

I'll let that feeling of relaxation and tiredness travel DOWN from my shoulders right DOWN my back *(Long pause for 5–15 seconds)*

And DOWN my right leg, DOWN through my muscles, DOWN through my knee, DOWN through my ankle … *(Pause for 1–3 seconds)*

To my foot, right DOWN to my toes *(Long pause for 5–15 seconds)*

I'll let that feeling of relaxation and tiredness now travel DOWN my left leg *(Pause for 1–3 seconds)*

DOWN through my muscles, DOWN through my knee, DOWN through my ankle… *(Pause for 1–3 seconds)*

To my foot, right DOWN to my toes *(Long pause for 5–15 seconds)*

I'll have a few moments now … *(Pause for 1–3 seconds)*

To allow me to concentrate on any part of my body that I would like to relax even further *(Pause for 15 seconds or longer if necessary)*

NB: When you begin the hypnosis you may find it easier to have a few sessions where you just repeat the above exercise, along with the termination section (at the end of the script) before you move on to deepening the exercise. If you suffer from smokers' cough, panic attacks or asthma do not breathe too deeply but take comfortable breaths.

Deepening

I want to concentrate on my breathing *(Pause for 1–3 seconds)*

I notice how every time I breathe out, I feel more and more relaxed *(Pause for 1–3 seconds)*

(Continued)

(Continued)

With each breath I take I feel so relaxed, so very, very relaxed *(Pause for 1–3 seconds)*

Breathe in slowly through my nose and slowly out through my mouth *(Pause for 1–3 seconds)*

With each breath I take ... *(Pause for 1–3 seconds)*

Every time I take a new breath of air ... *(Pause for 1–3 seconds)*

I am becoming more and more relaxed *(Pause for 1–3 seconds)*

On every out breath I become more, and more, sleepy *(Pause for 1–3 seconds)*

More and more deeply relaxed *(Pause for 1–3 seconds)*

I can notice how, as I relax, I am breathing more, and more, slowly *(Pause for 1–3 seconds)*

And more, and more, steadily, as I become more, and more, deeply, very deeply, relaxed *(Pause for 1–3 seconds)*

I am drifting DOWN into a deep state of relaxation *(Pause for 1–3 seconds)*

My whole body is becoming more, and more, relaxed, every time I breathe out *(Pause for 1–3 seconds)*

I am slowly going to count to five, and as I do, I will feel even more relaxed than I do now *(Pause for 1–3 seconds)*

One *(Pause for 1–3 seconds)*

NOW I am feeling more and more relaxed than I did a few minutes ago. More and more relaxed than I did a few seconds ago *(Pause for 1–3 seconds)*

Two *(Pause for 1–3 seconds)*

Notice how I am feeling so relaxed that I am finding it difficult to concentrate on my voice all the time *(Pause for 1–3 seconds)*

Three *(Pause for 1–3 seconds)*

(Continued)

(Continued)

Every time I say a number, every time I breathe out, I feel more and more deeply, very, very deeply relaxed. An overwhelming feeling of tiredness is descending upon me as I listen to my voice *(Pause for 1–3 seconds)*

Four *(Pause for 1–3 seconds)*

I am feeling even more relaxed now than I did a few minutes, a few seconds ago. In a moment when I say the number five, but not quite yet, I am going to feel so very deeply relaxed ... *(Pause for 1–3 seconds)*

NOW I feel even more relaxed than I did a moment ago, more relaxed than a few seconds ago, much more relaxed than I did a few minutes ago, and very much more than I did a few hours ago.

NB: You may want to have a few sessions incorporating the first two stages of the exercise plus the termination section (at the end of the script) before moving on to the final stage of self-hypnosis. In this part of the relaxation exercise, the aim is to drive home the positive effects of the hypnosis session outside the relaxation session.

Cognitive restructuring and stress management

I am now so relaxed, so very relaxed, that I am becoming very aware of what I am saying *(Pause for 1–3 seconds)*

I am so aware that my mind is open to any suggestions I may make for my benefit *(Pause for 1–3 seconds)*

I am feeling so relaxed that when I make positive suggestions about my health, I will accept these suggestions, and gradually over a period of time I will feel better and better, even though I will not be under self-hypnosis *(Pause for 1–3 seconds)*

My suggestions will just drift over my mind and I will be able to remember all the relevant ones that will positively influence my feelings *(Pause for 1–3 seconds)*

My behaviour ... *(Pause for 1–3 seconds)*

And my thoughts ... *(Pause for 1–3 seconds)*

(Continued)

(Continued)

As I feel more and more deeply relaxed during this session, I will find new energy to help me to cope with any problems I may have had recently *(Pause for 1–3 seconds)*

New energy to lessen any fatigue ... *(Pause for 1–3 seconds)*

New energy to help me concentrate on my goals ... *(Pause for 1–3 seconds)*

A new strength of mind and body to deal with internal and external pressures *(Pause for 1–3 seconds)*

I will become absorbed in life, my studies, and looking forward to every day *(Pause for 1–3 seconds)*

And as every day goes by, I will become more relaxed, and much calmer than I have been for some time *(Pause for 1–3 seconds)*

And each day, I will feel far less tense, and far less concerned with unimportant matters ... *(Pause for 1–3 seconds)*

And as this happens, my confidence will grow, as my old fears become a distant memory *(Pause for 1–3 seconds)*

Day by day, hour by hour, minute by minute, second by second, my independence is growing *(Pause for 1–3 seconds)*

Any stress, depression or anxiety or guilt will fade away as I learn to cope with life *(Pause for 1–3 seconds)*

I will learn to be able to stand difficult situations much more easily *(Pause for 1–3 seconds)*

I will no longer hear myself saying '*I can't stand it anymore*', but instead I will realistically say to myself '*I don't like it, but I stand it*' *(Pause for 1–3 seconds)*

I will see situations in perspective and not blow them up out of proportion *(Pause for 1–3 seconds)*

I will question whether things are really that bad *(Pause for 1–3 seconds)*

I will no longer wish to catastrophize events beyond reality *(Pause for 1–3 seconds)*

(Continued)

(Continued)

As I learn that I can stand situations, I will procrastinate less often and I will be able to start and continue my tasks more easily ... *(Pause for 1–3 seconds)*

And face my fears *(Pause for 1–3 seconds)*

If I fail at a task, I will not condemn myself as a failure or as stupid ... *(Pause for 1–3 seconds)*

All it means is that I did not achieve my target ... *(Pause for 1–3 seconds)*

No more, no less *(Pause for 1–3 seconds)*

I will learn to accept myself more for the person I am and not just for my achievements *(Pause for 1–3 seconds)*

My internal demands, many of those unnecessary musts and shoulds ... *(Pause for 1–3 seconds)*

... Will change to coulds and preferences and subsequently my stress and anxieties will lessen *(Pause for 1–3 seconds)*

Gradually, as time goes by, I will feel better and better and my life will improve ... *(Pause for 1–3 seconds)*

And my recent worries will be a thing of the past ... *(Pause for 1–3 seconds)*

And I will be able to put them behind me *(Long pause 5–15 seconds)*

In a few moments' time, but not quite yet, I am going to count to three and when I do, I will open my eyes and wake up, and feel relaxed and refreshed *(Pause for 1–3 seconds)*

I will be able to remember or forget whatever I want to of this session *(Pause for 1–3 seconds)*

And I will be in full control of my body and mind *(Pause for 1–3 seconds)*

As I count to three, I will wake up *(Pause for 1–3 seconds)*

One *(Pause for 1–3 seconds)*

Two *(Pause for 1–3 seconds)*

Three ... I can open my eyes in my own time.

Adapted from Palmer, 1993 © Palmer, 2006

Appendix 2
Useful Information

General

DirectGov
Website: www.direct.gov.uk/Topics/Learning/HigherEducationStudents/fs/en

British Psychological Society
St Andrews House, 48 Princes Road East, Leicester LE1 7DR
Tel: 0116 254 9568
Website: www.bps.org.uk
Holds a register of chartered psychologists

NHS Direct
Tel: 0845 4647

National Union for Students (London)
Nelson Mandela House, 461 Holloway Road, London N7 6LJ
Tel: 020 7272 8900
Text phone: 020 7561 6577
Email: nusuk@nus.org.uk

National Union of Students Scotland
29 Forth Street, Edinburgh EH1 3LE
Tel: 0131 556 6598
Email: mail@nus-scotland.org.uk

National Union of Students–Union of Students in Ireland
29 Bedford Street, Belfast BT2 7EJ
Tel: 028 9024 4641
Text phone: 028 9032 4878
Fax: 028 9043 9659
Email: info@nistudents.org

National Union of Students Wales (Undeb Cenedlaethol Myfyrwyr Cymru)
Windsor House, Windsor Lane, Cardiff CF10 3DE
Tel: 029 2037 5980
Email: office@nus-wales.org.uk

The Samaritans
The Upper Mill, Kingston Road, Ewell, Surrey KT17 2AF
If you are in crisis you can to the Samaritans: Chris, PO Box 9090, Stirling FK8 2SA
Use this web address to locate the closest Samaritans branch to you: http://www.
samaritans.org.uk/talk/local_branch.shtm
Tel: 08457 909090 (open 24 hours)
Email: Jo@samaritans.org

StudentsUK
Website: www.studentuk.com

Leaving the nest

Association for Rational Emotive Behaviour Therapy
PO Box 8103, Colchester, Essex CO5 9WL
Tel/fax: 01376 572 777 (general enquiries)
Website: www.arebt.org
Provides a list of accredited therapists who deal with stress, anxiety, phobias, panic
attacks and depression using rational emotive and cognitive-behavioural therapies

British Association of Anger Management
Tel: 0845 1300 286
Email: info@angermanage.co.uk
Website: www.baam.co.uk
Professional body of consultants, counsellors and trainers who offer individual
support, workshops, seminars and bespoke packages to assist with anger
management

British Association of Behavioural and Cognitive Psychotherapies
The Globe Centre, PO Box 9, Accrington BB5 0BX
Tel: 01254 875277
Fax: 01254 239114
Email: babcp@babcp.com
Website: www.babcp.org
Provides a list of accredited therapists who deal with stress, anxiety, phobias,
panic attacks and depression using cognitive-behaviour therapies

British Association for Counselling and Psychotherapy
1 Regent Place, Warwickshire CV21 2PJ
Information telephone line: 01788 578328
Website: www.bacp.co.uk
Provides a list of accredited counsellors and relevant organisations

Centre for Stress Management
156 Westcombe Hill, London SE3 7DH
Tel: 020 8293 4114
Website: www.managingstress.com
Provides stress counselling, coaching and training services and undertakes stress audits and interventions at work

Depression Alliance
Tel: 0845 123 2320 (all calls charged at the local rate)
Depression Alliance is a self-help organisation for people suffering from depression. It provides information, understanding and local self-help groups for the benefit of depression sufferers. Depression Alliance has three offices in the UK:

England
212 Spitfire Studios, 63–71 Collier Street, London N1 9BE
Email: information @depressionalliance. Org

Wales
11 Plas Melin, Westbourne Road, Whitchurch, Cardiff CF14 2BT
Email: wales@depressionalliance.org

Scotland
Depression Alliance Scotland, 3 Grosvenor Gardens, Edinburgh EH12 5JU
Email: info@dascot.org

International Stress Management Association
PO Box 348, Waltham Cross EN8 8XL
Tel: 07000 780430
Website: www.isma.org.uk
Provides information about stress management and accredits members

MIND
PO Box 277, Manchester M60 3XN

MIND *Information line*: 0845 766 0163 (Monday–Friday 9.15am–5.15pm). Deaf or speech-impaired enquirers can contact us on the same number (if you are using BT Textdirect add the prefix 18001).
Email: info@mind.org.uk
Mind is the leading mental health charity in England and Wales

United Kingdom Council for Psychotherapy
167–169 Great Portland Street, London W1W 5PF
Tel: 020 7436 3002
Fax: 020 7436 3013
Email: ukcp@psychotherapy.org.uk
Website: www.psychotherapy.org.uk
Holds a register of psychotherapists

Accommodation

StudentUK
Website: http://www.studentuk.com/Advice/accommodation.asp
Advice for student on finding and maintaining accommodation

The Student Village
Website: www.thestudentvillage.com
The student village aims to provide you with the highest standard and friendliest student halls available

Food for thought (nutritional information)

British Nutrition Foundation
High Holborn House, 52–54 High Holborn, London WC1V 6RQ
Tel: 020 7404 6504
Website: www.nutrition.org.uk

Eating Disorders Association
1st Floor, Wensum House, 103 Prince of Wales Road, Norwich NR1 1DW
National helpline: 0845 634 1414 (weekdays 8.30am–8.30pm, Saturdays 1pm–4.30pm)
Helpline email: helpmail@edauk.com
Website: www.edauk.com
Eating Disorders Association is a UK-wide charity providing information, help and support for people affected by eating disorders and, in particular, anorexia and bulimia nervosa. Details of local contacts in your area are freely available to callers ringing the national helpline

Foodfitness
Website: www.foodfitness.org.uk
The Food and Drink Federation's website offers healthy lifestyle tips and a self-assessment questionnaire on eating and exercise habits

National Centre for Eating Disorders
54 New Road, Esher, Surrey KT10 9NU
Tel: 01372 469493

Vegetarian Society
Parkdale, Denham Road, Altrincham, Cheshire, WA14 4QG
Tel: 0161 925 2000 (Monday–Friday 8.30am–5pm)
Email address: www.vegsoc.org
The Vegetarian Society is an educational charity promoting understanding and respect
for vegetarian lifestyles

Are you on the right course?

Centre for Coaching
156 Westcombe Hill, London SE3 7DH
Email: admin@centreforcoaching.com
Website: www.centreforcoaching.com
Provides coaching and guidance

DirectGov
Website: www.direct.gov.uk
Weblink: http://www.direct.gov.uk/Topics/Learning/HigherEducationStudents/fs/en
Information to help get you started in higher education: choosing a course, help
with applications and interviews, advice about student finance and graduate
careers

The Site.Org
Weblink:www.thesite.org.uk/workandstudy/studychoices/whatcourse/thewrongcourse
The site provides factsheets and articles on all the key issues, including sex and
relationships, drinking and drugs, work and study, housing, legal and finances, and
health and well-being

Managing your money

Consumer Credit Counselling Service
Wade House, Merrion Centre, Leeds LS2 8NG
Helpline: 0800 328 1813 (Monday–Friday 8am–8pm)
This is a dedicated helpline for students worried about debt and money problems.
Calls and advice given are free.
Website: www.cccs.co.uk

Department for Education and Skills
Link to details about student loans and financial support available: www.dfes.gov.uk/
studentsupport/students/index.shtml

Free Stuff
Website: www.freestudentstuff.com
A website containing free information and offers such as free cinema tickets, free
ringtones, cash for completing surveys, discount offers and much more *free stuff*!

Student Loans Company (SLC)
100 Bothwell Street, Glasgow G2 7JD
Tel: 0800 405010
Website: www.slc.co.uk

Relationships

British Pregnancy Advisory Service
Helpline: 08457 30 40 30 (action line for unplanned pregnancy)
Website: www.bpas.org

Family Planning Agency
2–12 Pentonville Road, London N1 9FP
Tel: 0845 310 1334 (9am–6pm, closed on Thursday 3pm–4.30pm)
Sexual health information line: 0800 567 123
Email: www.fpa.org.uk
Gives confidential information and advice on contraception and sexual and reproductive health. It also provides details of family planning clinics, sexual health clinics and other sexual health services elsewhere in the UK

Marie Stopes International
Helpline: 0845 300 8090
Website: www.abortion-help.co.uk

Relate
Relationships hotline: 0845 130 4010
Website: www.relate.org.uk
Relate is the UK's largest provider of relationship counselling and sex therapy. Relate offers advice, relationship counselling, sex therapy, workshops, mediation, consultations and support face to face, by phone and through the website

Drugs and alcohol

Alcoholics Anonymous
PO Box 1, Stonebow House, Stonebow, York YO1 7NJ
Helpline: 0845 769 7555 (24-hour service, calls charged at local rates, calls are redirected automatically to an AA member in your region).
Email: aanewcomer@runbox.com
Website: www.alcoholics-anonymous.org.uk

Alcohol Concern
Waterbridge House, 32–36 Loman Street, London SE1 OEE
Helpline: 020 7922 8667 (Monday–Friday 1pm–5pm)

Email: contact@alcoholconcern.org.co.uk
Website: www.alcoholconcern.org.co.uk
Gives information, guidance and advice for those worried about their own drinking habits or somebody else's. It also contains publications and a directory of local alcohol services

Drugline
Helpline: 020 8692 4975

FRANK
Helpline: 0800 77 66 00 (24-hour service)
Text phone: 0800 917 8765
Email: frank@talktofrank.com
Website: www.talktofrank.com
Offers free and confidential advice about any drug issue, whether it is information you require, advice or a chat. The website also contains facts, guidance and support information

Exploring your sexuality

London Lesbian and Gay Switchboard
Tel: 020 7838 7324 (24 hours)
Website: www.llgs.org.uk
Voluntary organisation that aims to provide a 24-hour telephone and referral service for lesbians and gay men

Outrage!
PO Box 17816, London SW14 8WT
Tel: 020 8240 0222
Website: http://outrage.nabumedia.com

Sexual Health Line
Tel. 0800 567 123 (24 hours)
Gives confidential advice and information about HIV and other sexually transmitted infections. Also provides information on where to find your local sexual health service

Students with disabilities

SKILL: National Bureau for Students with Disabilities
Chapter House, 18–20 Crucifix Lane, London SE1 3JW
Tel/Minicom: 020 7450 0620

Fax: 020 7450 0650

Email: skill@skill.org.uk

Information service: 0800 328 5050 (freephone) or 020 7657 2337(ringing on this number saves them money!) (Tuesday 11.30am–1.30pm and Thursdays 1.30pm–3.30pm)

Minicom: 0800 068 2422

Email: info@skill.org.uk

Promotes opportunities for young people and adults with any kind of disability in post-16 education, training and employment across the UK

Recommended reading

Buzan, T. (2003). *Use your Head.* London: BBC Books.

Cheeky Guides Limited (2002). *Cheeky Guide to Student Life.* Brighton: Cheeky Guides Limited.

Cooper, C. and Palmer, S. (2000). *Conquer Your Stress.* London: Chartered Institute of Personnel and Development.

Drew, S. and Bingham, R. (2004). *The Student Skills Guide.* Aldershot: Gower.

Neenan, M. and Dryden, W. (2003). *Life Coaching: A Cognitive-Behavioural Approach.* Hove: Brunner-Routledge.

Palmer, S., Cooper, C. and Thomas, K. (2003). *Creating a Balance: Managing Stress.* London: The British Library.

References

Alcohol Concern (2003). *Statistics on Alcohol and Health*. London: Alcohol Concern. Download from: www.alcoholconcern.co.uk

Association of University and College Counselling (2001). *Annual Survey of Counselling in Further and Higher Education 1999/2001*. London: AUCC.

BBC (2005). *Increase Your Sex Appeal*. Nottingham Features. Download from: www.bbc. co.uk/Nottingham/features/2005/5/smile_research.html

Becker, L. and Van Emden, J. (2004). *Presentation Skills for Students*. Basingstoke: Palgrave Macmillan.

Benson, H. (1976). *The Relaxation Response*. London: Collins.

Bernard, G. (2003). *Studying at University*. London: Routledge Falmer.

Birch, C. (1999). *Asserting Your Self*. Oxford: How To Books.

Bortner, R.W. (1969). A short rating scale as a potential measure of pattern A behavior. *Journal of Chronic Diseases*, 22: 87–91.

Buzan, T. (2000). *The Speed Reading Book*. London: BBC Worldwide.

Buzan, T. (2003). *Use Your Head*. London: BBC Books.

Cheeky Guides Limited (2002). *Cheeky Guide to Student Life*. Brighton: Cheeky Guides Limited.

Cooper, C.L., Cooper, R.D. and Eaker, L.H. (1988). *Living with Stress*. London: Penguin Health.

Cooper, C.L. and Palmer, S. (2000). *Conquer Your Stress*. London: Chartered Institute of Personnel and Development.

Cottrell, S. (2003). *The Study Skills Handbook*. Basingstoke: Palgrave Macmillan.

Dawson, C. (2004). *Learning How to Study Again: A Practical Guide to Study Skills for Mature Students Returning to Education or Distance Learning*. Oxford: How To Books.

Department of Health (2004). *The Score: Facts about Drugs*. London: HMSO.

Depression Alliance. (2004) *Students Stress Survival Pack*. London: Depression Alliance. Download from: www.depressionalliance.org/publications

Drew, S. and Bingham, R. (2004). *The Student Skills Guide*. Aldershot: Gower.

Ellis, A. (1977). The basic clinical theory of rational-emotive therapy. In A. Ellis and J.M. Whitely (eds), *Theoretical and Empirical Foundations of Rational-Emotive Therapy*. Monterey, CA: Brooks/Cole.

Evans, M. (2000). *Make Exams Easy: Learn Time-proven Exam Techniques, Boost Your Confidence and Results, Understand What Examiners Look For.* Oxford: How To Books.

Fitzhugh, K. (2004). *The Virgin University Survival Guide.* London: Virgin Books.

Friedman, M. and Rosenman, R.H. (1964). *Type A Behaviour and Your Heart.* New York: Knopf Wildwood House.

Lazarus, A.A. (1984). *In the Mind's Eye.* New York: Guilford Press.

Lazarus, J. (2000). *Stress Relief and Relaxation Techniques.* Chicago, IL: Keats Publishing Inc.

Lazarus, R.S. and Folkman, S. (1984). *Stress, Appraisal and Coping.* New York: Springer.

Longson, S. (2003). *Everything You Need To Know about Going to University.* London: Kogan Page.

Lusk, J.T. (1992). *30 Scripts for Relaxation, Imagery and Inner Healing.* Duluth, MN: Whole Person Associates.

McIlroy, J. and Jones, B. (1993). *Going to University: The Student Guide.* Manchester: Manchester University Press.

Milner, P. and Palmer, S. (1998). *Integrative Stress Counselling.* London: Cassell.

MIND (2003). *How to Cope with the Stress of Student Life.* London: MIND. Download from: www.mind.org.uk

MORI (Market and Opinion Research International) (2003). *Student Living Report.* London: UNITE.

MORI (2004). *Student Living Report 2004.* London: UNITE.

MORI (2005). *The Student Experience Report 2005.* London: UNITE in association with HEPI.

Neenan, M. and Dryden, W. (2003). *Life Coaching: A Cognitive-Behavioural Approach.* Hove: Brunner-Routledge.

NOP (National Opinion Polls) (2003). *Student Sex and Contraception Survey.* Evriwoman Survey. Download from: http://www.evriwoman.co.uk/survey/relationships.asp

O'Brien, D. (2003). *How to Pass Exams: Accelerate Your Learning, Memorise Key Facts, Revise Effectively.* London: Duncan Baird Publishers.

Palmer, S. (1989). The use of stability zones, rituals and routines to reduce or prevent stress. *Stress News*, 1(3): 3–5.

Palmer, S. (1993). *Multimodal Techniques: Relaxation and Hypnosis.* London: The Centre for Stress Management and Centre for Multimodal Therapy.

Palmer, S. and Dryden, W. (1995). *Counselling for Stress Problems.* London: Sage.

Palmer, S. and Neenan, M. (1998). Double imagery procedure. *The Rational Emotive Behaviour Therapist*, 6(2): 89–92.

Palmer, S. and Strickland, L. (1996). *Stress Management: A Quick Guide.* Dunstable: Folens Publishers.

Palmer, S., Cooper, C. and Thomas, K. (2003). *Creating a Balance: Managing Stress.* London: The British Library.

Ranzetta, L., Fitzpatrick, J. and Seljmani, F. (2003). *Megapoles: Young People and Alcohol.* London: Greater London Authority.

Rosenman, R.H., Brand, R.J., Jenkins, C.D., Friedman, M., Straus, R. and Wurm, M. (1975). Coronary heart disease in the Western Collaborative Group Study: final follow-up experience of 8.5 years. *Journal of the American Medical Association*, 22: 872–7.

Stewardson, N (2004) *W2K–Reaction–Health.* Download from: www.clients.thisischeshire. co.uk/w2kreaction/boys_n_toys/health_alcohol.html

The Times (2001). The Energy Plan: Parts 1 & 2. *The Times*,

Index